The *ULTRALIGHT* BACKPACKER

The Complete Guide to Simplicity and Comfort on the Trail

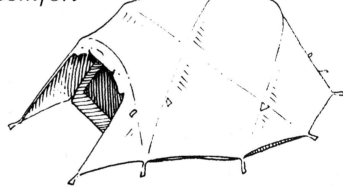

Ryel Kestenbaum

RAGGED MOUNTAIN PRESS / McGRAW-HILL

Camden, Maine • New York • Chicago • San Francisco • Lisbon • London • Madrid •

Mexico City • Milan • New Delhi • San Juan • Seoul • Singapore • Sydney • Toronto

Ragged Mountain Press

A Division of The McGraw-Hill Companies

10 9 8 7 6

Copyright © 2001 Ragged Mountain Press
All rights reserved. The publisher takes no responsibility for the use of any of the
materials or methods described in this book, nor for the products thereof. The
name "Ragged Mountain Press" and the Ragged Mountain Press logo are trade-
marks of The McGraw-Hill Companies. Printed in the United States of America.

Library of Congress Cataloging-in-Publication Data
Kestenbaum, Ryel.
  The ultralight backpacker : the complete guide to simplicity and
comfort on the trail / Ryel Kestenbaum.
      p.   cm.
Includes index.
ISBN 0-07-136828-0
1. Backpacking. I. Title.

GV199.6.K47 2001
796.51—dc21   2001001480

Questions regarding the content of this book should be addressed to
Ragged Mountain Press
P.O. Box 220
Camden, ME 04843
www.raggedmountainpress.com

Questions regarding the ordering of this book should be addressed to
The McGraw-Hill Companies
Customer Service Department
P.O. Box 547
Blacklick, OH 43004
Retail customers: 1-800-262-4729
Bookstores: 1-800-722-4726

This book is printed on 70 lb. Citation at R.R. Donnelley, Crawfordsville, IN
Illustrations by Christopher Hoyt
Photographs by Ryel Kestenbaum except where otherwise indicated
Design by Dede Cummings Designs
Production by Dan Kirchoff and Eugenie S. Delaney
Edited by Tom McCarthy and Don Graydon

The ULTRALIGHT
BACKPACKER

*"After you have exhausted what there is in business,
politics, conviviality, love and so on—have found
that none of these finally satisfy, or permanently
wear—what remains? Nature remains."*

—*Walt Whitman*

To the memory of my father,
who always took the trail less traveled.

CONTENTS

PREFACE

THE DRIVING PRINCIPLE BEHIND THIS book is that lighter is better. Ultralight backpacking is the natural embodiment of this premise in the realm of nature. Every day, people are proving that going ultralight is an easy, safe, and enjoyable way of experiencing the wilderness.

Traditionally, backpackers have given a lot of attention to gear, making sure that they're adequately prepared for any possible situation. The common thinking is that anything less severely compromises personal safety. I wrote this book partly to move away from this undue reliance on gear and to shift the emphasis to our own instincts and common sense. My research, my talks with backpackers, gear designers, and manufacturers, and my own experiences on the trail have shown me the benefits of ultralight backpacking.

Still, many people haven't yet experienced it for themselves. I continue to see backpackers looking like soldiers going off to battle, with huge packs and bulletproof tents and piles of clothing. But that's not what being in nature is all about. It's about feeling free, unbounded, shedding the distractions and barriers of our built-up world.

Of course, no one wants to be a slave to their gear. Most people would much prefer to shed the pounds and travel light. Maybe you've even had dreams of skipping along a trail with a featherweight pack on your back, humming and wishing that life could be like this all the time. Well, I have good news. However you came to pick up this book and begin reading, I'm going to say one thing that I hope will keep you going to the very end: there has never been a better way to enjoy the wonders of nature than ultralight backpacking, and there has never been a better time to give it a try.

During the research and writing of this book, I came to realize something that I hadn't quite grasped before. Rather than just being an easy, simple way of venturing into the wilderness, ultralight backpacking is really a profound culture, a way of life that can simplify the complications of our environment. It can be a way of discovering what we really need in order to be happy and complete, whether it's on a hiking trip in the Sierra high country or on the trail of life itself. You can immerse yourself in the pursuit of ultralight backpacking as much or as little as you want, yet always come away with something useful and wonderful.

Whatever your reason for spending time in the wilderness, I hope this book helps you attain a deeper appreciation for it and a stronger connection with it. Ultralight backpacking has welcomed thousands already, and now I welcome you as well. So, take a couple days off, strap on your ultralight pack, and get yourself out into nature.

I hope to see you on the trail.

ACKNOWLEDGMENTS

IN RESEARCHING AND WRITING THIS book, I was very fortunate to have around me so many patient, supportive and discerning people. Those that I mention here are representative of many others that time and space limit me from thanking by name.

On the administrative side of things, Tom McCarthy and all the folks at Ragged Mountain Press have exhibited nothing short of top-notch professionalism and talent. Tom, thanks for your intuitive guidance and support in making this a book that I am so proud of. I am also deeply grateful to Betsy Amster whose invaluable insight and thoroughness make her one of the best. I also thank Don Graydon for his editing skills.

All the stunning models you see in these pages are not professionals, but my old colleagues at Adventure 16. They are Cory Freyer, Dave Fleischman, Marmot, Kier Stiteler, John Reyher, Lauren Abrahams, and Joshua Zilm.

If I can indulge in just one cliché among these acknowledgments, I'd like to say that this book certainly would not have been possible without the direction and wisdom of Noel Riley Fitch, from whose group the first seed of this book began to grow. In the same vein, I am indebted to James Ragan and his inspiring vision realized in the Master of Professional Writing program at the University of Southern California.

I extend my deepest appreciation and love to family and friends whose reassurances and encouragements carried me through the process. Becky, thank you for your confidence in me; I won't ever forget it. And Mom, now you can finally carry the book around under your arm.

Lastly, I gratefully acknowledge the countless backpacking mentors, students, partners, and acquaintances who have walked along the trail with me, and all the ones I have yet to meet.

INTRODUCTION
THE ULTRALIGHT WAY

A COMMON PHILOSOPHY AMONG backpackers seems to be: "It's better to have something and not need it than to need something and not have it." The idea appears to make sense. But the more you think about it, the more you realize it's really only appropriate if you're stuck on a desert island. For modern backpackers, it just serves as an excuse to load up with everything you need and a lot you don't.

Ray Jardine, one of the first ultralight backpackers, was a lot closer to the mark when he said, "If you don't have it, you don't need it."

It's not necessary to prepare for every conceivable scenario you might encounter in the outdoors. All you need for survival and contentment are the essentials—which we'll discuss later on—aided by your own common sense. I'm talking about the old-fashioned common sense that tells you that you don't need to pack gear for a two-day trip to Yosemite as if you're going to Everest. This transition from relying on gear to relying on ourselves is the seed from which ultralight backpacking sprouts.

Ultralight travel remains a somewhat controversial concept in the backpacking community. Dissenting opinions are still voiced as each person clings to his or her own tried-and-true method of getting out into nature. But the ultralight approach continues to attract new adherents. Manufacturers have also gotten on board, introducing new equipment designed with the ultralight backpacker in mind.

People embraced backpacking long ago as a way to experience nature on its own terms. Yet the ties to home are hard to cut. You still see backpackers whose goal seems to be to carry along all the comforts of home. But much of the lure of walking in the wilderness is precisely because it's *not* like home. And this is where ultralight backpacking enters the picture, as a way to help us adapt to nature rather than the other way around.

1

PILLARS OF THE ULTRALIGHT WAY

Throughout this book, I'll introduce concepts that form the pillars of ultralight backpacking. They can be summed up in a single maxim: Simplest is best, and best is lightest. These basic concepts are:

- The smaller the pack, the less weight you'll have to carry. Essentials go in, luxuries stay out.

- Every last fraction of an ounce counts. Don't let even the smallest extra weight hitch a ride on your back.

- Every item must earn its place in your pack. Judge the necessity of each item against its weight, then decide whether you really need to bring it.

- The fewer barriers you have between yourself and the outdoors, the more in touch you become with nature, and the more you are able to appreciate it.

It is this last concept that I would like you to remember the most. It is why I wrote this book and why I keep returning to the wild places, time after time.

These concepts govern the entire book, beginning with the first chapter, which scrutinizes backpacks and explains what to look for in an ultralight pack. Backpacks that weigh in at less than 3 pounds? You'll find them here. The chapter on shelter judges the merits of ultralight tents, tarps, and bivy sacks. Chapters on sleeping bags and clothing and other gear also lay out methods for reducing the weight of each and every item you carry down the trail—and which items can best be left at home. We'll cover every-

thing from footwear to underwear, from water filters to toothbrushes.

After that, much of the book is devoted to your health and well-being. Separate chapters identify foods that work well for the ultralight backpacker, discuss ways to stay in good health while in the wilderness, and provide techniques for walking and breathing. You'll also find information and lots of advice on long-distance hiking.

One chapter explores another key element: the ultralight state of mind. As you adopt the techniques of going ultralight, you'll discover that it involves more than just wearing a light pack. Let's face it: no matter how much you learn from this book, your own mind has to be on board for any of it to be successful for you. The goal of the chapter is to help you train your mind to see nature through the eyes of an ultralight backpacker—to adopt the ultralight state of mind.

WHY ULTRALIGHT?

As the name states, ultralight backpacking is a way to travel light, unburdened by excess weight. Going ultralight reduces the weight of your backpack and its contents to the smallest possible amount, while still providing for the necessities.

Traditional backpacking has long been guided by a rule that says a pack should not weigh more than a third of your body weight. For the average-size male, this amounts to almost 60 pounds. Sound like fun? Maybe for five minutes, if you don't move too much, but just try walking a few miles and see how you feel.

Now, here is the beautiful truth of ultralight backpacking: by using its techniques and equipment, you can reduce the weight of your loaded pack to 15 pounds, and even 10 pounds or less (excluding food and water). It's possible to get it down to not much more than the weight of an average college knapsack.

Of course, the longer your hike and the more extreme the environment, the heavier will be your pack. But even then, the same techniques will save you many pounds, and could mean the difference between pain and pleasure. When I started a hike that took me 250 miles up the Pacific Crest Trail, my pack weighed about 20 pounds. Some people have hiked the entire trail with packs that weighed between 10 and 15 pounds, relying along the way on resupply points.

The benefits don't stop at merely saving weight. The lighter load will free up your muscles to serve you more efficiently, meaning you can cover greater distances and see more. Or you might reach your campsite sooner and have more time to explore the area.

Backpackers sometimes suffer from a condition known as *plantar fasciitis*—a painful inflammation of the plantar fascia, the thick connective tissue that runs from heel to toe at the bottom of each foot and helps support the arch. Putting too much weight on it time after time can result in microscopic tears where the tissue meets the heel, which leads to sharp projections of new bone (heel spurs) that can make the pain unbearable.

Carrying loads of 50 or 60 pounds on backpacking trips is a sure way to treat this loyal companion badly. The best bet for preventing inflammation and pain is to reduce the weight on your feet. Keeping your total

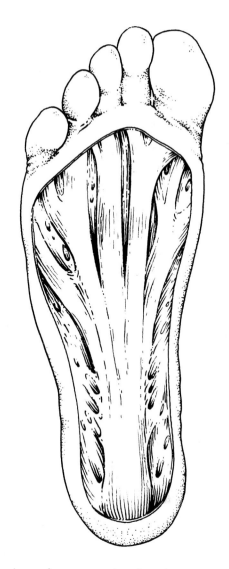

The plantar fascia: your best friend, or sworn enemy.

backpacking weight down can help make it possible for you to walk 20 miles a day, day after day, on feet that remain strong and healthy. They may feel sore at the end of a long day, but by the next morning, they should be ready for the trail once again.

Then there's the lower back, which

assumes much of the weight of a heavy pack. When the spine has to endure extended periods of heavy pressure, there's a danger that the discs separating the vertebrae might eventually slip or rupture. Again, the answer is a lighter pack.

Because your center of gravity moves rearward when you carry a pack, you must tilt your torso forward to compensate. This action puts increased pressure on the lower back. By going ultralight, you are able to walk with a more upright stance, which further relieves tension on the back.

Other parts of your body that will thank you for switching to ultralight are your ankles, knees, hips, and every other joint. Gravity is a mighty force that should be respected, but it will leave you mostly unharmed if you give it as little substance as possible upon which to exert its force.

If you have never backpacked, the biggest obstacle between wherever you are and the heart of the backcountry may have nothing to do with muscles or vertebrae. It may simply be the fear of the unknown. Ultralight backpacking offers a means of allaying that sort of fear. It's a way of making your adventures into the wilderness easy and uncomplicated.

When you travel light, you may find yourself backpacking with fewer worries and less stress, with more time and energy to enjoy the trip. Why? Because you've pared the contents of your pack, and the headaches of gear-tending, down to the essentials. You've simplified.

With less weight on your back and fewer worries on your mind, you'll be able to devote your attention to the things that attracted you to the wilderness in the first place. The ultralight way offers an opportunity to fully immerse yourself in the beauty and harmony of nature.

CHAPTER 1
BACKPACKS

L ET'S JUMP RIGHT INTO THE HEART OF ultralight backpacking, to the one object that can be your best friend or your worst enemy: the backpack itself.

Along with the telephone, the computer, and countless other items in our lives, the backpack has shrunk significantly over the years. The volume of a full-size, vintage-1970s backpack could hit 7,000 cubic inches. Into this cavernous abyss you would toss clothes, food, tent, stove, sleeping bag—and for good measure, some extra food "just in case," more clothes in the event of an arctic blizzard, and random stuff that you might perchance need somewhere along the trail, and because half of the pack is still gaping empty, some books, lawn furniture, and a teddy bear.

Compare that with one of my ultralight packs: the Osprey Aether 36, with its thrifty capacity of 2,400 cubic inches—not much bigger than the average college knapsack. The amazing thing about this smaller pack is that I still carry clothes, food, tent, stove,

and sleeping bag—and maybe, just maybe, a book or two.

You can still buy a huge pack, but you don't have to. It's just a matter of selecting the smaller pack that's right for you. And of course the smaller a pack is, the more thoughtful you have to be with what you put in it, thus ending up with a lighter load.

Before we continue, let me mention that we're restricting our discussion of backpacks to those with an internal-frame design, or no frame at all. External-frame packs have long had the reputation of being able to carry heavy loads better than anything else. But since we're not concerned with heavy loads or how to carry them, you can rule out any need for an external-frame pack.

I have to confess that the first pack I purchased was a monstrous 5,500-cubic-inch internal-frame model that the manufacturer claimed was ultralight only because its 6-pound weight was 2 pounds lighter than the next pack up the line. That's 6 pounds with nothing in it! Six pounds is practically half the weight of a serious ultralight back-packer's fully loaded pack.

I took this pack and experimented with cutting and trimming many of the external frills that served no purpose except to make me look cool as I hiked down the trail, straps bouncing around me. When I finally put the scissors down, I ended up with 1½ pounds of extraneous material. A 4½-pound pack is still about two pounds too heavy, but the experiment proved to me that scissors can be an ultralight backpacker's most useful tool.

THE RIGHT FIT, THE RIGHT FEEL

A pack that fits properly and weighs little will ride so well you might forget you have it on. It becomes an extension of your own body so that your movements while wearing it remain fluid and intuitive. Any veteran skier, surfer, or hang-glider pilot will tell you their equipment is as much a part of them as their arms or legs, and so it should be for you as an ultralight backpacker.

Of course, you won't experience this deep connection simply by trying on a pack in the outdoors store and wearing it around for a few minutes. But you'll be able to get a good idea of which pack is right for you. The well-fitting pack rides close to the body so that there is complete contact throughout. After all the adjustments have been made, the pack should feel like it's hugging you from behind. The hip and pelvic structure is by far the most efficient part of the skeleton for carrying weight, so at least two-thirds of the fully loaded pack should be discernibly resting on your hips.

Experiment with different settings of the

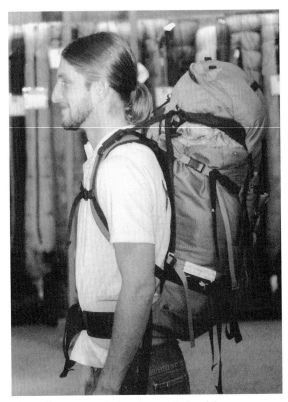

This is how a pack that fits well should appear from the side: the shoulder straps curve comfortably over the shoulders, the waist belt is positioned directly over the hips, and the pack makes even contact with the back along its entire length.

various straps to attain the best fit. Most packs have the same five kinds of basic adjustment straps, which should be adjusted in the following order: waist, shoulder, stabilizer, load-lifter, and sternum. Ultralight packs, however, often dispense with some of these adjustments.

The waist belt should rest right over your hip bones so that the buckle ends up about an inch below the belly button. The easiest way to cinch down a waist belt is to put your right hand on the right side of the buckle and

And from the front: the sternum strap is positioned comfortably over the chest, the shoulder straps are on the inside part of the shoulder and terminate about two inches below the armpit, and the waist belt buckle is just below the navel.

pull the right strap across with your left hand, and then vice versa with the left strap.

Pull the shoulder straps until they become taut.

The stabilizer straps go from the base of the pack to the waist belt. Pull these tight so that most of the weight is shifted to your hips.

The load-lifter straps, terminating on top of the shoulders, bring the whole pack closer to your back. As with the shoulder straps, pull these until they are taut.

The sternum strap pulls the shoulder straps toward each other a little bit so that they aren't resting on the sensitive nerves and tissue of the outer shoulder. The sternum strap should rest across your sternum.

As you adjust each strap, you'll notice that the pack gets a little more comfortable each time. But if you get all the straps dialed in and the pack still applies uncomfortable pressure to a shoulder or a part of your back, try a different model or brand. Each manufacturer has a different idea of how a pack should fit. Even if one pack feels like a dream, try on others to get a better idea of the difference between a good and a bad fit.

You'll notice that in general, the smaller the pack, the fewer adjustments it will have. The advantage of this is that there are fewer things to fiddle with and fewer things to go wrong. On the other hand, if a particular part of your body starts acting up, there are fewer options for adjusting the pack to help relieve the problem.

Once you hit the trail, you'll need to readjust the pack occasionally as the terrain changes, as different parts of your body tire, and as the weight of your loaded pack changes over the course of a trip (for instance, getting lighter as your food supply diminishes).

Make sure you get a pack that's correctly fitted for your torso. Packs come in different sizes (Small/Medium/Large or Short/Regular/Tall), so try on various models in different sizes until you find one that contours around your back and shoulders correctly. Don't discount capacity when selecting a pack: a size Small has a lower capacity than a size Large of the same pack, up to 1,000 cubic inches in some cases.

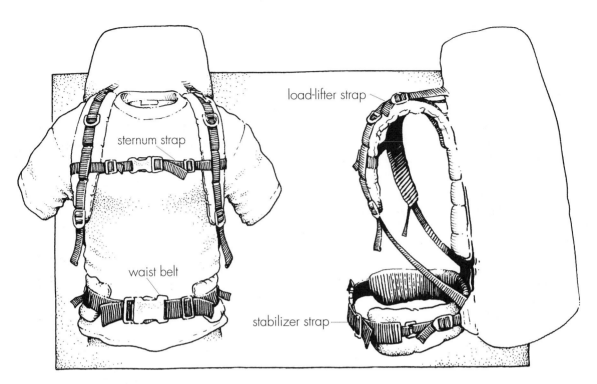

A pack's other adjustments.

Most internal-frame packs use either aluminum or fiberglass stays as part of the suspension system. Some packs have a single stay, which runs along your spine, while others have two that run along the sides of the pack. Some of the smaller, lighter packs don't have stays at all. Once you have a pack that fits well, pull out any stays so you can fine-tune them to your back.

Have a friend help you bend and align the stays so they contour along your back. Once they are dialed in, slide them back into the pack and try it on again. The pack should make contact along the complete length of your back. If it doesn't, keep adjusting the stays as necessary, or try a different pack.

LIGHTWEIGHT BACKPACKS

When you're ready to go light, you have two broad options in choosing a pack. You can take the full plunge and insist on only the smallest and lightest of backpacks (discussed in the next section). Or you can start with something a bit less intimidating: a medium-size pack in the range of 3,500 to 4,500 cubic inches, weighing in at about 3 to 4½ pounds. They may not be pure ultralight packs, but they can still be considered lightweight and are certainly a step in the right direction.

Buying the roomier model can be a good decision if you're just starting out and aren't yet entirely comfortable trusting me and my 2,400-cubic-inch pack. It's also a good deci-

THE ULTRALIGHT WAY: THE STRAP-DIARRHEA TEST

Not a pretty picture: all those messy straps and buckles and loops dangling from an otherwise handsome pack. Is this another pack suffering from strap diarrhea?

Manufacturers have come to believe that the more technical a pack looks, the more appealing it is to a customer. As a result, many packs—especially in the medium to large range—are burdened beneath pounds of mostly nonessential fittings and features.

As you consider a pack, try giving it the strap-diarrhea test. Pick the pack up by the loop at the top of the pack between the shoulder straps. Hold the pack out away from you and rotate it quickly in the air. If a tangle of straps bounces and slaps back and forth as you rotate the pack, set it down and move on; the pack gets a failing grade.

Try this with several packs. You'll soon learn which packs suffer from strap diarrhea, gussied up with more extraneous material than any ultralight backpacker would ever need. Put these packs back on the rack and leave them for the technophiles.

Granted, this is a subjective exercise, mainly to get you thinking about which straps are necessary and which aren't. You'll likely discover that many packs fail the strap-diarrhea test. The manufac-

The Strap-Diarrhea Test: Hold the pack by the top loop and twist vigorously.

turer's marketing department apparently believes a pack should be different from what the customer actually needs, an approach that's common with products today. The public doesn't seem to mind this dichotomy, as evidenced by the ubiquity of four-wheel drive vehicles on the streets of Beverly Hills and Miami Beach.

sion if you are backpacking in colder climates and need to take bulkier insulating items. Or maybe Uncle Bob gave you his old backpack—and we all know a free pack can work pretty well no matter what the size.

You'll find that some of these packs are top-loading only, while others are both top-loading and panel-loading, with an extra opening on the front of the pack. This extra panel can be an attractive option, but it adds considerable weight, so restrict your search to top-loaders. Look for packs that are simple in design and function. After all, a backpack is simply a bag for holding your gear;

it doesn't have to solve mathematical equations. Fewer straps, buckles, and zippers mean a lighter pack.

Following is a list of packs you might consider. All these capacities and weights are for the medium size of each particular model. Of course, you may not always find these models, because pack designs come and go. But this list gives you an idea of some of the packs that do a good job of keeping weight reasonable while providing a relatively generous capacity, and doing it with clean and durable design.

- Osprey Aether 60 (3,700 cubic inches; 3 lb., 2 oz.)
- Marmot Front Point (4,000 cubic inches; 3 lb., 6 oz.)
- Mountainsmith Auspex (4,200 cubic inches; 3 lb., 14 oz.)
- North Face Prophet (3,700 cubic inches; 3 lb., 15 oz.)
- Arc'teryx Khamsin 62 (3,800 cubic inches; 4 lb.)
- Dana Design Bridger (4,000 cubic inches; 4 lb., 7 oz.)
- Gregory Gravity-X (3,850 cubic inches; 4 lb., 7 oz.)

> *The smaller the pack, the less weight you'll have to carry. Essentials go in, luxuries stay out.*

One of the lightest packs in this general range is the modular Arc'teryx Nozone, a 3,400-inch pack designed primarily for rock

The Osprey Aether 60. *Courtesy Osprey*

climbing but adaptable to backpacking. It weighs just 2 pounds, 6 ounces when converted to its minimum form.

The Speed pack from Dana Design uses an interchangeable system of stuff sacks that can be attached to the 2-pound, 2-ounce suspension and frame. This system lets you select from among many sizes of stuff sacks so that the practical range of cubic-inch capacity is enormous.

THE ULTRALIGHT BACKPACK

Ultralight packs embody the very core of ultralight backpacking. But to use such a pack as the container for everything you need requires a considerable leap of faith. You must trust yourself to be able to get along without all the extras you might throw into a larger pack.

Let me first pose a question: which is the better ultralight pack, one that weighs 2 pounds and has a capacity of 3,000 cubic inches, or a hypothetical pack that weighs the same 2 pounds but has 5,000 cubic inches? Your first thought might be the roomier pack, since it gives you more freedom to take the things you want to have with you. But then consider that a fully loaded 3,000-inch pack weighs far less than a fully loaded 5,000-inch pack. And therein lies one of the pillars of the ultralight philosophy: The smaller the pack, the less weight you'll have to carry. Essentials go in, luxuries stay out.

So, just what is an ultralight backpack? I consider an ultralight to be a pack that weighs less than 3 pounds, with a capacity that is usually not much more than 3,000 cubic inches, and sometimes considerably less. It's a pack that is light, small, and simple to use; it isn't burdened with technical-sounding gadgetry; it keeps pads, straps, zippers, buckles, loops, tabs, and flaps to a minimum.

An ultralight pack requires that you establish some limits on its use. It's probably not the best pack for an expedition to the Alaska bush. But it will work pretty well for two weeks along the John Muir Trail in the High Sierra of California or for a short backpacking trip in your local mountain range. Along with some good common sense, you can even use an ultralight pack to hike the entire 2,100-mile Appalachian Trail. The pack will work even better if you travel with other people,

sharing some of the gear that you would otherwise be carrying on your own.

Let's examine some of the features of an ultralight pack. Right away, you'll notice how much simpler it is. No superfluous straps here. The waist belt and shoulder straps won't be as padded and heavy as those on a larger pack—primarily because the pack designer assumes you won't be carrying as much weight and hence won't need as much support. There probably won't be any stabilizer straps or load-lifter straps, mostly for the same reason.

You won't find any internal stays in these ultralight packs. The only thing that separates your back from the inside of the pack

Notice the absence of load-lifter and stabilizer straps. The fist technique (see pages 14–15) has yet to be performed on this particular pack.

might be the nylon material of the pack itself, perhaps augmented by a foam pad. As you can see, the light weight of the smaller pack isn't only a function of its smaller size, but also of the fact that less material is needed to beef up its support structure.

After taking a look at some of the highly padded, feature-laden packs on the market, you might fear that an ultralight will be the most uncomfortable thing you've had on your back since the time that bookcase fell on you. But as any scientist will tell you, the simplest answer is usually the right one. In our case, the simplest pack is the lightest pack and is usually the most comfortable one.

There's also a cost advantage. The ultralight packs are often cheaper than their larger counterparts, because they require less material and fewer worker-hours to manufacture.

A beautifully simple ultralight pack that is produced for the mass market is the Osprey Aether 36. I use the large size of this particular model for my ultralight trips. It weighs about two and a half pounds after you've trimmed the excess strappage from it (see Trimming the Fat, below), and it has a capacity of 2,400 cubic inches. With a little sweat, I've managed to fit everything in it that I need for a four-day backpacking trip, and more if I'm resupplying along the way.

Following are a few of the other packs that also fit the ultralight description well. The capacities and weights are for the medium size of the particular pack model.

- Camp Trails Gemini (2,540 cubic inches; 2 lb., 2 oz.)
- Lafuma Extreme 42 Light (2,600 cubic inches; 2 lb., 4 oz.)
- Mountainsmith Ghost (3,000 cubic inches; 2 lb., 6 oz.)
- Arc'teryx Khamsin 38 (2,500 cubic inches; 2 lb., 7 oz.)
- Madden Approach (2,500 cubic inches; 2 lb., 9 oz.)
- Wild Things AT Pack (1,800–5,000 cubic inches/frameless; 2 lb., 9 oz.)
- Rokk Paramint (2,500 cubic inches; 2 lb., 14 oz.)
- North Face Prophet 45 (2,750 cubic inches; 3 lb., 1 oz.)

The GoLite Breeze is a 3,000-cubic-inch pack that can be extended up to 4,200

The North Face Prophet 45. Courtesy North Face

inches—and weighs only 11 ounces. However, to have a pack this light, you give up a hip belt, sternum strap, compression straps, and a top lid. This pack is a viable option only if what you are carrying is extremely lightweight. For any load of more than 10 pounds or so, I want at least some sort of hip belt.

GoLite also produces the Gust, which it calls a climbing pack but can be used for carrying heavier loads than the Breeze because it includes a hip belt. The Gust, at 1 pound, 3 ounces, has a capacity of 3,600 cubic inches.

One of the lightest mass-produced backpacks on the planet is the Kelty Cloud 4000. Its capacity is 3,500 cubic inches—but it weighs just a single pound, thanks in part to its extremely lightweight Spectra material. The drawback—there has to be at least one for something this light—is the cost. The pack, made from the very expensive Spectra fiber, costs $550. But if price is no concern, the Cloud 4000 is definitely a pack to consider. It also uses a modular approach to design, allowing you to customize the components of the pack to reflect the kind of trip you'll be taking.

TRIMMING THE FAT

The general rule in designing internal-frame packs seems to be the more straps and fancy features, the better. You'll encounter such components as internal and external compartments, dual aluminum or fiberglass internal stays, foam lumbar pads, gear loops and slings—and enough compression straps to secure the load on a dozen backpacks. I call this the Medusa backpack.

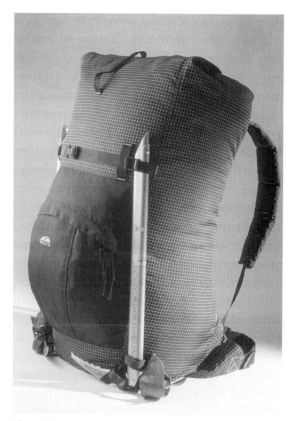

The GoLite Gust. Courtesy GoLite

We have a choice on this issue. We can stick to that minority of packs that take a simpler approach—such as the true ultralight packs discussed in the preceding section—or we can apply some creative trimming to our lightweight but strap-happy packs. Here's how to be creative.

First take a deep breath and remind yourself that once you own a product, you can change it in any way you like. It's amazing how reluctant we are to alter something after we've spent our hard-earned money on it, as if we believe a pack will fall apart or lose some hidden quality if we so much as snip an inch from one strap.

The next step is to grab your scissors and cut off the ice-ax loops. These loops are found at the base of the pack. Next, attack the lash tabs. They are usually located on the topmost part of the pack and are used to attach even more stuff—just in case you can't cram everything inside.

Then check for any flaps and pockets inside the pack. Many packs include an interior flap that separates the sleeping bag compartment at the base of the pack from everything above —basically, a two-bedroom backpack. Just tell yourself that everyone can be more social in a one-bedroom backpack, and add that flap to the growing pile of material snipped from the bag.

Some packs also have a large pocket on the inside of the pack, ostensibly to be used for a water bladder. Out it comes. (One useful feature you might want to keep is an internal compression strap, which tightens everything down inside once the pack is full.)

The top lid of some backpacks converts into a fanny pack for taking side trips from your campsite. But if you're using a stuff sack for your clothing or sleeping bag, it can serve double-duty for these day trips: I've always been able to shove what I need into my pockets or into a stuff sack that I carry in one hand. Even if you like the idea of having a fanny pack, you likely won't regret losing it

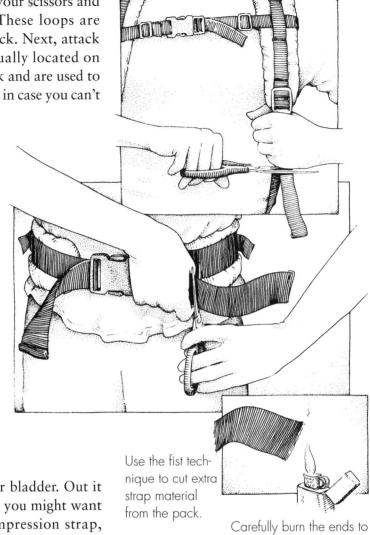

Use the fist technique to cut extra strap material from the pack.

Carefully burn the ends to prevent fraying.

when you see how much material is used to make the top lid function as a fanny pack. If you have a "floating" top lid, you can remove it simply by undoing the straps. But if you need to cut the straps to remove the top lid, think carefully before you do it; once it's gone, it's gone for good.

Now comes the fun part—what I call the *fist technique*. It's a way to shorten straps to the lengths you actually need. Start by loosening every single strap on the pack. Load it up with anything that will fill it fairly lightly. Pillows work pretty well. Now tighten the compression straps as much as you think you'll need for an actual load, and then make a fist around the loose end of each strap, as close to the pack as possible. For these straps, allow an extra inch beyond what's in your fist, and cut off the remainder. With a lighter, burn the edge of the cut so that it won't fray.

> *Every last fraction of an ounce counts. Don't let even the smallest extra weight hitch a ride on your back.*

Once all the compression straps are taken care of, go ahead and put the pack on. Now tighten all the various adjustment straps. Your pack may have all five of the most common adjustment straps: waist, shoulder, stabilizer, load-lifter, and sternum. Adjust these straps until the pack fits comfortably. Using the fist technique again, cut off all that extra strap material—but this time cut it off right at the end of your fist. (The adjustment straps don't require that extra 1-inch allowance that we gave to the compression straps.)

By now you should have accumulated a considerable pile of scrap—and the pack looks cleaner, neater, and simpler. You can celebrate by weighing the pile to see how much weight you've saved.

This is a good time to remember another pillar of ultralight backpacking: Every last fraction of an ounce counts. Don't let even the smallest extra weight hitch a ride on your back. Even if an adjustment strap pro-

THE ULTRALIGHT WAY: LIGHTEN UP

If your pack has internal stays, experiment with using the pack without the stays. It's sometimes possible to remove these aluminum or fiberglass stays without sacrificing the fit or comfort of the pack.

trudes only half an inch beyond your fist, do away with that half-inch. Once you start telling yourself, "Oh, it's only a fraction of an ounce," those fractions start adding up very quickly. Being zealous with every ounce is good training for learning to think as an ultralight backpacker. Eventually you'll reach the point where every time you look at a pack, in a store or on someone's back, you will automatically see all the ways to reduce its weight.

HOW TO PACK A PACK

The guidelines on packing a pack are much the same no matter what kind of container you end up strapping to your back. The idea is to maintain a balanced center of gravity. If you load the pack with most of the weight near the bottom, your shoulders will end up bearing the bulk of it. If the heaviest weight is at the top, you'll be inclined to tip over whenever you tilt your upper torso away from vertical. If the weight sits too far from your center of gravity, you'll know it as soon as you take a step. The goal is to integrate the pack seamlessly into your stride and stance.

Stuff Sacks

Before you begin loading the pack, it's a good idea to separate some items into stuff sacks. They're a wonderful invention that can be used for a multitude of purposes, not the least of which is to prevent items from sliding to the bottom of the pack. Use the lightest stuff sacks for your purposes, and as small as you can get away with. Some people get a little stuff-sack crazy and have a dozen of them floating around the pack. But as an ultralight backpacker, try to use as few as possible.

Here we come to another of the pillars of the ultralight philosophy: Every item must earn its place in your pack. Judge the necessity of each item against its weight, then decide whether you really need to bring it. Even with something as light as a stuff sack, you have to ask yourself: Do the benefits of the sack outweigh its weight? If not, don't use it.

On occasion I've backpacked without stuff sacks, and it can be an enormous inconvenience to have everything loose inside the pack. So I accept an extra ounce or so in exchange for a hassle-free packing experience. Some people do backpack without any stuff sacks at all, and that approach is definitely worth considering. Not only do you save weight, but you can also use your gear to fill in every little bit of space. No matter how tightly you shove in your stuff sacks, there will always be some dead air space around the corners.

The maximum number of stuff sacks I now use is two: one for clothes and one for food. Many people also use a stuff sack for the sleeping bag. Of these three, the stuff sack for clothing should usually be the smallest and the one for food the largest.

Zippered Plastic Bags

Zippered plastic bags, such as the Ziploc brand, are another fantastic invention. They come in all sorts of shapes, sizes, and thicknesses, and they become airtight and watertight when sealed.

I learned the hard way about the benefits of zippered plastic bags. On one of my first backpacking outings, I threw all my toiletries into the top pocket of my pack. On the third day, I began to notice a strange minty odor. I discovered that my bottle of liquid soap had ruptured, spilling its contents down into the pack itself, permanently staining my tent and clothes. I've used zippered plastic bags ever since and have never had a repeat experience of the busted bottle.

In one oversize, freezer-duty bag that I keep in the top pocket, I put toothbrush, tooth powder, spoon, bug repellent, sunscreen, candle, waterproof matches, and liquid soap. If any container leaks, I only have to clean the offending contents from the other items in the bag. These bags also work well to keep other things isolated.

These bags are also great for carrying food after you've removed it from its commercial packaging, saving both weight and space. But as with anything else in your pack, don't bring more bags than you truly need.

Loading It Up

An important rule of packing is to maintain an even, symmetrical weight. Looking at a pack from the rear, imagine a vertical line running down the middle of it; then try to keep both the left and right sides of the line weighing about the same. Your body works most efficiently, and happily, when it is symmetrically weighted.

Before you load your pack, lay everything out in front of you. Keep a checklist of everything you need, and double-check that it's all there. Now loosen all the pack's compression straps. Start by loading your sleeping bag into its place at the bottom of the pack. You may need to engage in a little shoving and shifting to get the bag to sit squarely across the bottom so that each end is jammed tightly into the bottom corners of the pack. If you decide against using a stuff sack, keep pressing down on the bag until it is as compressed as possible. The advantage of going without a stuff sack is that you'll more easily be able to fill every little bit of space.

> *Every item must earn its place in your pack. Judge the necessity of each item against its weight, then decide whether you really need to bring it.*

Next, shove in your shelter, whether it's a tent, tarp, or bivy sack. It doesn't need a stuff sack; just jam it right into the pack and press it down as far as it will go. Don't bother trying to fold your shelter neatly, since folding creates lines of weakness that can eventually lead to tearing. Use the shelter's material to fill in any empty spaces left over from the sleeping bag.

Next comes the stuff sack that carries your clothes. Lay this horizontally across the pack and press it down as far as you can.

Between the clothing stuff sack and your back, place your water bladder. Put it in upside down so that gravity can provide an uninterrupted flow, and bring the hose up and out the top of the pack.

Fuel bottles and fuel canisters are tricky items to pack because they won't bend to conform to the inside of the pack. If you have an MSR-type fuel bottle that looks sort of like a soda bottle, you can stow it vertically right next to the water bladder, being sure to maintain a symmetrical weight between the two. If instead you are using a gas canister, which is more round in shape, simply stuff it down into any space that looks like it can accept it.

Last in is the food. Food occupies the space at the top of the pack, where you have the easiest access to it. To help keep items from shifting, put the heaviest food items at either end of the stuff sack. The stove and pot also go into the food sack. Nest the stove inside the pot to conserve space.

If rain is in the forecast, I keep my rain gear above my food, for quick access. Your sleeping pad can go inside the pack if the pad is compactable enough. Slide it in along the inside edge of the pack, or put it just above your sleeping bag.

Now cinch everything down with the pack's internal compression strap, if it has one. Then pull the drawstring tight. In the pack's top pocket goes the zippered plastic bag with toiletries, along with such items as maps, utility cord, first-aid kit, knife, tent stakes, and a snack.

On the outside of the pack, use the external straps to tie down the tent poles (if you're using a tent) and sleeping pad (if it's not already inside the pack). Many packs have either a large strap or flap that extends upward from the bottom of the pack—very useful for carrying your sleeping pad or wet rain gear. When it's impossible to fit everything inside the pack, you can get away with using this flap or other straps to stow gear. Just bear in mind the need for weight symmetry. The farther away the gear is from your back, the more you'll have to fight an offset center of gravity.

The packing system I've laid out is just one way to do it. Experiment with different approaches until you find the one that's most comfortable for you. Many people pack their food lower down and their clothes higher up. Others put nighttime clothing lower down, with daytime clothing higher, where it is more accessible. Some place their water bladder flat across the pack rather than vertically. There are no hard-and-fast rules, except to keep the center of gravity as balanced as possible.

Once everything is loaded up, tighten the compression straps, which will bring the whole weight of the pack closer to the center of gravity and reduce its overall bulk.

Putting It On

Before you don the pack, loosen all the adjustment straps. Lift the pack and swing it onto your shoulder. Once it's on, tighten and adjust all the straps in the proper order: waist belt first, then shoulder straps, stabilizer straps, load-lifter straps, and lastly the sternum strap. Ultralight packs can make the job easier, because many of them don't include stabilizer or load-lifter straps.

Once everything is adjusted, feel for a sense of weight symmetry. Sway back and forth and side to side, and swivel your hips, trying to feel for any imbalance. If you find any, readjust the straps. If that doesn't work, you'll have to remove the pack and relocate some of its contents. Once the pack feels even and symmetrical, you're ready to hit the trail.

Walking with a backpack usually feels unnatural at first, but you'll find that eventually your body and mind adapt. The smaller and lighter the pack, the more natural it feels when you first strap it on. A lightweight or ultralight pack allows your body a freer and more natural range of motion.

As you hike, use the adjustment straps to compensate for any discomfort. If your hips start to ache, loosen the waist belt and tighten the shoulder straps or sternum strap. If one shoulder is bothering you, loosen the corresponding shoulder strap and take up the slack with the other one. Fine-tuning a pack is a constant endeavor, and you'll find that eventually you'll do it naturally.

CHAPTER 2
SHELTER

IN THE REALM OF BACKPACKING, A shelter serves only a handful of practical purposes. Essentially it's just a piece of nylon that keeps you out of the rain and away from the bugs. But if there's no rain and no bugs, why add that extra weight to your pack?

Campers have made a habit of setting up their tents even if the skies are perfectly clear and the only bug is of the Volkswagen variety back at the trailhead parking lot. I believe the reason for this is that we've become so attached to the notion of privacy that we feel we must create a private space wherever we go by climbing into a tent that cuts us off from the beauty we've come to enjoy. So before we launch into a discussion of tents and other forms of shelter, let's first address this issue.

Here's a scenario: you're preparing for a two-day backpacking trip, and you're trying to keep things ultralight. The weather forecast says there's little chance of rain, and the likelihood of encountering bugs is small. Do you pack a tent? Let's further assume you

have no reason to fear intruders, either human or animal. Can you still justify those two or three or four extra pounds of weight?

I've slept without any form of shelter except the sky above me many times, in all parts of the country and in a variety of conditions, and I've never been molested, attacked, bothered, or abused. In fact, sleeping in the open air with nothing but the stars and the trees for cover has always been a deeply satisfying and rewarding experience.

This leads us right to another pillar of ultralight backpacking. In fact, it is the central pillar that supports all the others: The fewer barriers you have between yourself and the outdoors, the more in touch you become with nature, and the more you are able to appreciate it.

Of all the various physical and mental barriers that prevent us from achieving a harmonious unity with the natural world, the tent is among the easiest to remove.

Of course, if there is any chance of foul weather or a swarm of locusts striking near

The best tent is none at all, under the open sky.

you, some kind of shelter might come in handy. There are basically three choices: tents, tarps, and bivy sacks. Which you choose depends on where you're going, what time of year it is, how many people you are traveling with, and other variables. Back-packers have hiked the entire 2,600-mile Pacific Crest Trail with just a tarp to shelter them, and others have weathered winter storms in Alaska with nothing more than a waterproof bivy sack. Let's start with tents.

TENTS

Tents come in all shapes and sizes, fabrics and designs, colors and features. Some consist of little more than a nylon sheet suspended above and around you, while others have multiple bedrooms and take three days to set up. The selection of tents can be overwhelming.

It's easy to buy a tent that far exceeds your needs. The first few times I went out alone, I carried a three-person, 8-pound palace of a tent. I thought the extra space might be nice if I just wanted to lounge around. After struggling up and down hills for hours, cursing every ounce of that tent, I ended up lounging around a lot more than I had anticipated. But at least I had my acres of purple and gray real estate to make me feel better.

> *The fewer barriers you have between yourself and the outdoors, the more in touch you become with nature, and the more you are able to appreciate it.*

Backpacking tents generally come in two flavors: three-season and four-season. As to which season is not included in the three-season tent, I'll give you one guess, and spring, summer, and fall don't count. Four-season tents are aimed at people who will be exposed to the harshest conditions Mother

Nature can throw at them. If you're going on a two-week winter expedition in the Himalayas, you're going to need a four-season tent, just as you would hiking in the Cascades in January. But since we're dealing here with ultralight backpacking and not winter mountaineering, let's concentrate on three-season tents.

A handful of tents fall under a so-called summer-season category. These tents consist of little more than mosquito netting (also known as *no-see-um* netting), with nylon for a base. They don't provide any protection from the elements, however, so we won't consider them either.

As ultralight backpackers, we want the lightest three-season tent that still offers adequate protection from the weather. We need only enough space for our sleeping bag and various accouterments, and maybe a small vestibule for our shoes and pack. Inside a tent, I want to be able to sit up, eat, change clothes, and stretch. The ideal tent is one that allows you to do these things while still being as light as possible.

In selecting a tent, you'll need to consider whether you want one that is freestanding or nonfreestanding, and whether it will be of double-wall or single-wall design.

Freestanding vs. Nonfreestanding

A freestanding tent is one that can be erected without using any ground stakes. A system of tent poles (most commonly of aluminum or fiberglass) run through sleeves or clips to give the tent its shape and stability. The poles are tensioned against the sleeves or clips, which are attached to the fabric of the tent itself. Almost all dome-style tents are freestanding.

THE ULTRALIGHT WAY: LEAVING HOME

A general rule about outdoors products is that the more comfortable they are, the heavier they are. Nowhere does this apply more than with tents. Some tents try too hard to duplicate the luxuries of home. They're massive, loaded with features, and burdened with a multitude of storage pockets in every wall. The perfect home away from home.

Embracing ultralight backpacking can liberate us from our conventional views of luxury and comfort. All we need from a tent is protection from the elements and from bugs. That's it.

You can set the freestanding tent up just about anywhere that's fairly flat, including on rock. If you don't like where it sits, just pick it up and move it.

The problem is that freestanding tents are almost always heavier than the nonfreestanding variety. As you might guess, I prefer the nonfreestanding tent, because of its considerable savings in weight. Besides, these tents are every bit as good and useful as freestanding models, and staking out a tent is no big deal—especially when you realize that even a freestanding tent needs to be secured so that it doesn't blow away. One quick gust of wind will turn a $400-freestanding tent into the most expensive kite you've ever bought. For this reason you'll need to stake it to the ground, or at least tie it to a tree or large rock.

If you are traveling with one or two other

hikers, it may be possible to justify the extra weight of a freestanding tent. As a rule, two-person freestanding tents should weigh less than 5 pounds, and three-person models less than 8 pounds. Nonfreestanding tents are almost always designed for either one person or two.

Double-Wall vs. Single-Wall

For many years, tent designers have grappled with the problem of how to make a tent waterproof while at the same time allowing the moisture of your breath and perspiration to escape so it doesn't condense on the inner walls of the tent. If they fail, you end up with condensation dripping relentlessly down on you.

The problem is that when you try to solve one half of the puzzle, you make the other half worse. If your tent is waterproof, rain can't get in—but then there's no way for your own bodily moisture to escape, and it's going to end up on the walls and eventually on you and your gear. On the other hand, if you use a tent fabric that isn't waterproof, your body moisture can escape but the rain gets in.

You could try using a waterproof tent, and leaving a door or window open to ventilate interior moisture—but then you're likely to have the worst of both worlds: some body moisture still condenses, and some rain still gets in.

The double-wall tent is the best system that designers have been able to produce so far to keep you dry from all forms of moisture. Nearly all backpacking tents use this construction.

The double-wall tent uses a breathable, nonwaterproof inner wall that incorporates plenty of mesh windows and doors so that your breath and perspiration can pass through to the outside. The separate outer wall is completely waterproof. The outer wall *(rainfly)* is made of the same nylon or polyester as the inner wall, but is coated with a waterproofing material. (Incidentally, a polyester fly works better than nylon because it doesn't stretch and sag when wet.)

The tent is set up with a separation of a few inches between the inner wall and the rainfly as a space through which moisture can escape. This separation is critical; if the rainfly touches the inner wall, interior moisture can't escape. I don't know how many times I've woken up to find that the moisture-laden fly has collapsed onto the inner wall, rendering the tent useless at keeping me dry.

If you can afford it, buy your tent from one of the top manufacturers. The tent will cost more than a Wal-Mart special, but the design and materials will be far superior, and you'll stay a lot drier.

Now we come to the tent equivalent of the auto-show "concept car," the single-wall tent. Only a handful of such tents are available, partly because of their high cost and partly because they don't necessarily work as well as you might expect. But they've been around for a while, ever since the advent of waterproof-breathable fabrics, the most famous of which is the ubiquitous Gore-Tex.

The basic premise of Gore-Tex and other waterproof-breathables is that water vapor can pass through the fabric in one direction, but water can't pass through in the other direction. In principle, the waterproof-breathable fabrics were born to be used in a

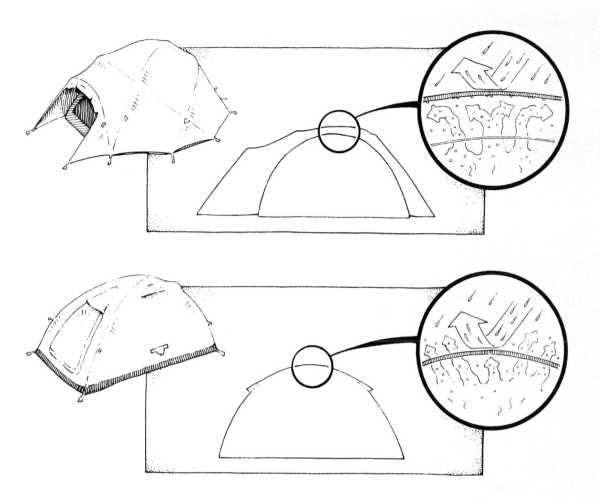

Double-wall and single-wall tent construction.

tent, because they should be able to solve the basic tent dilemma: how to let moisture from your sweat and breath escape while keeping you dry in the rain.

The problem is in the fine print. Gore-Tex relies on letting water vapor pass to the outside *only* when there is a temperature differential between one side of the fabric and the other. If both sides are the same temperature, the fabric won't work as intended. Since there is so much space between your perspiring skin and the Gore-Tex wall of the tent, the fabric can't perform nearly as well as it would if it were in your jacket or sleeping bag, where it would be right next to your warm skin.

Another problem is that the fabric must be unobstructed in order to let out the moisture from the inside. If raindrops stick to the outside of the fabric, then water vapor can't escape. You'll wake to find yourself lying in a small puddle of your own sweat. If you open a door or window for ventilation, there's no rainfly to keep out the rain.

The only time I would consider a single-wall tent is if I believed the weather would stay dry for my entire trip. But in that case I wouldn't take a tent at all.

Tent Features

Your tent should have certain features that bring it closer to the ideal ultralight tent. Look for these features before deciding which tent is right for you.

Bathtub Floor. The best tents incorporate a "bathtub floor," where a single piece of fabric is used to create the floor and first few inches of the walls. Because there is no seam in the floor, water can't seep up from beneath the tent. Floor seams can be protected with seam sealer, but this material does wear off.

Lightweight Poles. Tent poles are almost always made of aluminum or fiberglass, although a few tents offer weight-saving, though expensive, carbon fiber poles. Almost all higher-end tents use aluminum poles, which are equally strong in any temperature, unlike fiberglass poles, which lose strength in very cold weather. When sections of an aluminum tent pole are joined, they present a smooth, uninterrupted surface. Fiberglass sections, on the other hand, are joined with ferrules, metal housings that add an unwelcome protrusion at the joints.

You can save weight on poles by buying a tent that uses either shorter or thinner poles. Shorter poles usually mean a more constricting tent; thinner poles mean less strength. But my dual-hoop tent uses poles that are both short and thin, and they haven't broken yet. If you can afford it, consider carbon fiber poles, which are lighter than any others.

Clips or Sleeves? One of the perennial debates among backpackers is over the best device for attaching poles to the tent. Some say clips; others say sleeves. I prefer tents that use clips, because the clips allow for a greater flow of air between the rainfly and the tent. Sleeves are usually made with some kind of mesh material, but even then they hinder the flow of air that is crucial to having a well-ventilated tent.

Fans of tents that incorporate sleeves point out that a pole within one of the long sleeves exerts a more evenly distributed tension on the tent than a pole held by a few clips. Why this particularly matters, I don't know, since I've never seen a clip rip from the tent. Also, I've found that tent poles tend to snag on the sleeve material as you are threading them through.

Vestibule. The vestibule is similar to a cabin's mud room—a place where you can kick off your dirty shoes and change clothes before clambering into the tent. It's also a place to keep your pack, your dog, or extra gear. If it's raining, you can cook in the vestibule. Vestibules are formed by an extension of the rainfly, creating a protective awning that is usually secured by staking it out.

On my one-person tent, the rainfly is staked out about 4 feet from the door so that it comes down from the larger tent hoop at a 45-degree angle to form the vestibule. I have found it to be indispensable; I would be very hesitant to ever get a tent that didn't have a vestibule.

The clip option for tent poles.

The covered sleeve option for tent poles.

Stakes. Stakes for your tent or tarp need to be only about 6 inches long. Nothing is lighter than titanium stakes, and nothing is more expensive, either. Otherwise, go with metal stakes. Those rounded stakes with the hook at one end that come with new tents are next to useless; they bend easily, and then it's Frustration City trying to get them straight again, so always use right-angled stakes.

THE ULTRALIGHT TENT

Following are a few suggestions for quality ultralight tents. They're almost all of the proven double-wall design.

Nonfreestanding Tents (Double-Wall)

If you are traveling alone or with someone you don't mind sharing small spaces with, there are some fine tents to choose from. The dual-hoop tunnel design seems to have proven itself as the best lightweight style. A large hoop curves over your head, and a smaller hoop curves over your feet.

These tents come in both one-person and two-person versions. Look for a one-person tent that weighs less than 3 pounds, or a two-person tent that weighs well under 5 pounds. It's also possible to fit two people into a one-person hoop tent. In the Yosemite backcountry, I several times shared a one-person REI SoloLite with a partner. Despite the intimate quarters, the tent worked perfectly well. The tent's weight, when split between the two of us? A whopping 1 pound each.

Dual-hoop designs differ a bit in dimensions, weight, cost, and how you get in and out of them—but overall there's not a lot of variation. Here are a few one-person and two-person dual-hoop tents that I've tried and like (but understand that not all these models may continue to be available, since new designs are always evolving):

- Sierra Designs Ultra Light Year (1-person; 2 lb., 8 oz.; 20 sq. ft.)

- Walrus Zoid 1.0 (1-person; 2 lb., 14 oz.; 20 sq. ft.)

- Mountain Hardwear Solitude (1-person; 3 lb., 2 oz.; 19 sq. ft.)

- Walrus Zoid 1.5 (2-person; 3 lb., 9 oz.; 26 sq. ft.)

- Sierra Designs Clip Flashlight (2-person; 3 lb., 10 oz.; 32 sq. ft.)

- Mountain Hardwear Trinity (2-person; 4 lb., 6 oz., 37 sq. ft.)

- Kelty Windfoil Ultralight (2-person; 4 lb., 6 oz.; 41 sq. ft.)

An unusual but attractive option is the Dana Design Javelina, which uses your trekking poles for setting it up, rather than regular tent poles. The Javelina weighs only about 2 pounds, and at 31 square feet can be used as either a roomy one-person or a tight two-person shelter.

Freestanding Tents (Double-Wall)

There are no suitable freestanding ultralight tents made for just one person, so I'll concentrate in this section on freestanding tents for two people. For a two-person, freestanding tent to qualify as ultralight, I want it to weigh no more than 5 pounds, and these all qualify handily.

The Mountain Hardwear Solitude (with fly, right).
Courtesy Mountain Hardwear

Many freestanding tents include three or more poles, obviously a weighty feature, but ultralight tents are often designed with only two. Two poles weigh less than three, but they won't provide as much tent stability in bad weather.

One of my favorite ultralight tents is the North Face Slickrock—perhaps the only exception to the general rule that freestanding tents outweigh their nonfreestanding cousins. The Slickrock weighs in at only 4 pounds, 1 ounce. Of course there's a trade-off: if you're taller than about 5-foot-10, your feet and head will hit the walls when you're lying down. You also get only a partial rainfly.

The Mountain Hardwear Tri-Light 2 is a two-person tent that uses three poles that meet at a unique three-way attachment. But you still have to put up with a tight (or cozy, depending on the occupants) fit. The Mountain Hardwear Approach weighs a little more, but you get more space in return. Following are a few recommended tents, includ-

The Marmot Nutshell.
Courtesy Marmot

The two-person Bibler I-tent weighs 3 pounds, 12 ounces. Interior space is only 27 square feet, and if you are taller than 5-foot-10 or so, you are going to have to sleep diagonally or scrunched up. The tent can be a hassle to set up, since you have to run the poles through sleeves that are on the inside of the tent. Bibler uses its proprietary ToddTex waterproof-breathable material, which seems to have had better success than other such fabrics in single-wall tents.

The Kelty Dart is a single-wall tent that doesn't use waterproof-breathable fabric at all. It simply employs a waterproof material and a design that allows for plenty of venti-

ing the Slickrock and the two Mountain Hardwear models (square footage includes vestibule).

- North Face Slickrock (4 lb., 1 oz.; 31 sq. ft.)

- Mountain Hardwear Tri-Light 2 (4 lb., 1 oz.; 39 sq. ft.)

- Marmot Nutshell (4 lb., 10 oz.; 36 sq. ft.)

- North Face Rainier (4 lb., 11 oz.; 33 sq. ft.)

- Mountain Hardwear Approach (4 lb., 12 oz.; 40 sq. ft.)

- Kelty Assault (4 lb., 12 oz.; 37 sq. ft.)

Single-Wall Tents

Although I'm not a fan of single-wall tents, let me mention a couple of models that have gained some popularity among ultralight backpackers.

Remember Mr. Miyagi and his bonsai tree? Look at your gear in the same way, always searching for its inner ultralight essence.

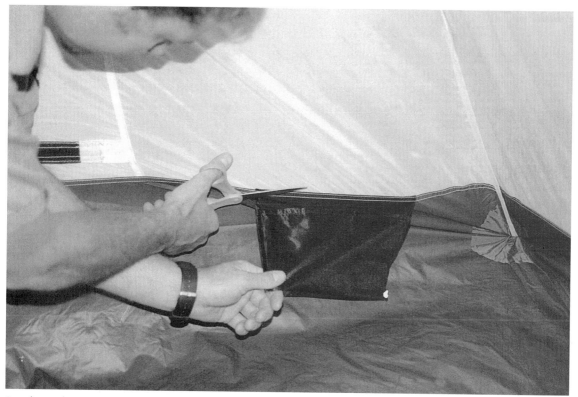

Break out the scissors to remove any unnecessary material from the tent, like these pockets.

lation. The result is a light, economical tent that won't work quite as well as one using a waterproof-breathable fabric. The one-person Dart 1 weighs 2 pounds, 4 ounces, while the two-person Dart 2 weighs 2 pounds, 12 ounces.

Another single-wall tent that does not employ waterproof-breathable fabric is the Marmot Area 51, a two-person model that weighs 5 pounds.

TRIMMING THE FAT

It's time to play everyone's favorite game, "Fun With Scissors." That's right, sharpen your scissors, because your new tent is begging for its fat to be trimmed off. Before we begin, set up the tent. Then throw away the stuff sack, or save it for use as a Christmas stocking.

If you have ever watched *The Karate Kid*, you'll know that Mr. Miyagi is an ultralight backpacker. There is a scene in the movie where he is poised before a bonsai tree, clippers in hand, visualizing how the tree should look in its most beautiful state. Somewhere within the tree lies its true self, just as somewhere within the tent that you have set up before you lies the perfect ultralight shelter.

Ultralight is a state of mind: try to visualize the tent as the lightest, simplest, cleanest possible form it can take. Take a walk around the tent, looking for anything that takes away from this vision. You'll likely see clips, straps, buckles, and fasteners of every kind. If you crawl inside, you might see pockets, zipper tassels, and more fasteners.

Now take a deep breath and start in on the things that have the least function. Those interior storage pockets can go, as can all the extra strap material that you use to tighten the edges of the rainfly to the stake.

On the side of the door are fasteners to secure it when it is open. If you really can't bear to lose these fasteners, leave one and cut off the others. Slice off the zipper tassels. Carefully remove the manufacturer's label, if there is one sewn to the tent. Remove any tags that are attached to the tent.

By now, you should have accumulated a little pile of cut-off material that represents a few precious ounces shaved from the weight of the tent. You might find yourself feeling surprisingly good about it all. You may have subtracted only a small amount of weight, but there is something about revealing the true ultralight form in your tent that just feels right.

TARPS

A tarp is nothing more than a sheet of waterproof material that is suspended above the ground in some manner. There are no poles, no zippers, no rainfly, no windows or doors, and no gadgetry to make it complicated. Because of its admirable simplicity and its consequent weight savings, a tarp has been the shelter of choice for many ultralight backpackers. However, with tent designs and materials becoming ever lighter and more technologically advanced, there are fewer reasons for using tarps. Still, tarps are definitely lighter and more compact than just about any tent out there. They will save you precious ounces.

Tarps require a good bit of patience to set up. Just try pitching a tarp in a brisk wind. I used a tarp on a portion of the Pacific Crest Trail, and although it kept me dry (mostly dry, anyway) and made my pack lighter, I finally switched to a one-person tent that weighed about a pound more. The hassle of setting the thing up, along with its greater exposure to the elements, eventually made me rethink my shelter strategy enough that I was able to justify that extra pound. There were several nights when the sky hurled rain at my tarp, and the rivulets that formed during the night ensured that I woke up soggy.

However, it's possible to fit two people under a tarp that weighs 2 pounds or less, and I wouldn't hesitate to use one with a partner if the conditions were appropriate. If you and your partner really want to keep the weight and bulk down, you can't do much better than sharing the weight of a tarp.

A tarp has other distinct advantages over a tent, the most significant one being superior ventilation. The only way you could have a better-ventilated shelter than a tarp is to use nothing at all. Air is guaranteed to circulate, which is useful if you ever end up with a traveling partner like the one I endured during an Outward Bound trip. He had yet to master the art of backcountry hygiene and developed a powerful odor that enveloped anyone in the immediate vicinity. If I and my other two tarp-mates had been

This tarp-tent was homemade by Chuck Mohr of Idaho.

sleeping in a tent, we would surely have been asphyxiated.

The fanciest feature you'll find on a tarp is a nice variety of pretty colors. Very little can go wrong with a tarp. With tents, the poles can break, zippers can get caught, the seams can deteriorate, and so on, but a tarp is so simple that only a major tear in the fabric would render it unusable. Even if the guyline attachments break or a corner is ripped off, a tarp can still function adequately.

A tarp is also very versatile. You can rig it in different ways, depending on your needs. In a strong wind, you can angle the tarp to help ward off "the flaps," that maddening flapping of tent fabric. You can ele-vate one side to allow more ventilation, or you can bring one end right down to the ground to make the inside less susceptible to rain. If the sky goes from clear blue to a full-on monsoon in ten seconds, you can whip out the tarp and get yourself under it in eight. You might not be able to get it fully rigged, but you'll stay a lot drier than if you had to take the time to wrestle with a tent.

Another benefit of tarps is that they allow you to fire up the stove and not risk burning your house down, since a tarp has large openings with lots of fresh air coming through. You can set up the stove right inside the entrance and cook dinner even if it's rain-ing. (You should never light a stove inside a tent, although an open vestibule area just outside the tent can be used for that purpose—with care.)

A backpacking tarp should be about 8 feet wide by 8 feet long. Most tarps are made of either nylon or polyester, coated with polyurethane. The tarp must have *grommets*—metal rings with holes—sewn into the tarp along the edges so you can attach guylines. You want at least a grommet at each corner and halfway along each side. Some of the better tarps will also have guyline attachment points closer to the middle so that you can anchor the tarp with greater security in heavy winds.

You'll also need a groundsheet—the only thing simpler than a tarp. It is made of some form of plastic, usually polyethylene. Some of the more durable groundsheets are made of nylon and have a Mylar coating on one side. Cut the groundsheet to fit around your sleeping pad. A groundsheet weighs next to

nothing if it is kept clean. Give it a good shake every morning, and fold it so any remaining dirt or moisture is on the inside.

A commercial variation in tarp design—the Black Diamond Megamid—uses a single pole to hold up the middle of the tarp, making it look much like a tepee. The Megamid can sleep four people and weighs only 3 pounds, 8 ounces.

A new breed of tarp that is rapidly gaining favor is called the tarp-tent—essentially a tarp that incorporates some material, usually lightweight netting, that hangs down to form an enclosed space. A tarp-tent combines the simplicity of a tarp with the protection of a tent, without adding more than a few ounces to the total weight.

The GoLite Cave and Nest, a two-piece design, works in this way. The two pieces together weigh 1 pound, 13 ounces for the two-person version. Mountain Hardwear has its own one-piece variation in the two-person Bat Ray 2, weighing 2 pounds, 14 ounces. The Bat Ray is essentially a tarp with walls that hang down from the edges of the tarp.

BIVY SACKS

A bivy sack is basically a waterproof shell for your sleeping bag. The bivy is extremely light and compact, and gives you and your sleeping bag practically complete protection from moisture. Like most single-wall tents, a bivy sack is made of waterproof-breathable fabric, most commonly Gore-Tex, with a water-proof—but nonbreathable—section for the base. The most simple design has a zipper along the side and a zipper or vent over your head.

A little higher on the luxury scale are bivies with some kind of pole design that props the top portion above your head and upper chest. Top-of-the-line bags are just a hair removed from being small single-wall tents. The Bibler Tripod, for example, uses the familiar dual-hoop design, albeit with much shorter poles, and an additional pole that extends from the top of the upper hoop to the ground behind your head. It provides enough room to read a book or to stave off

The GoLite Cave and Nest shelter system. The separate tarp and tent sections can be combined to form a lightweight shelter. Courtesy GoLite

Mountain Hardwear Ethereal Bivy.
Courtesy Mountain Hardwear

claustrophobia for a bit longer than in smaller bivy sacks, but the added weight doesn't really justify its use.

One advantage of a bivy sack is that you can jump right into it and set it up from the inside if it's raining. Of all the various choices for shelter, a bivy is by far the easiest to assemble—even easier if no assembly is required, as is the case with no-pole bivies.

Of course, since there's no room for your pack inside, you and your sleeping bag may be the only things dry by morning. A simple solution is to bring along an oversize garbage bag and put your pack in it. You can also line the inside of the bivy sack with your clothes and other essentials that you don't want to get wet.

Given the choice between a bivy sack and a tarp that both weighed the same, I'd have to go with the tarp. You can fit all your gear beneath its generous ceiling, and in a steady rain, you're more likely to stay dry. Many bivy sacks can eventually let moisture seep

through, and once it does, your sleeping bag becomes a big, wet rag.

With a tarp, you have the option of cooking under cover, which you obviously can't do when the ceiling is a few inches above your nose. And tarps are a lot cheaper than bivies, which can be unbelievably expensive considering what you get.

Perhaps the biggest negative about bivy sacks is that they offer relatively little interior ventilation, despite the "breathable" part of their material. And last, but certainly not least, if you suffer at all from claustrophobia, the confining quarters of a bivy sack are most definitely not for you.

With all that said, however, I still have a bivy sack on standby at home. I take it on overnighters when I feel lazy and don't want to deal with setting up a tarp or tent, and when there is little chance of a storm.

If you think a bivy sack would suit your needs, you can check out some of the quality choices recently on the market. Bibler offers the Hooped Bivy and the Tripod Bivy, both of which use its proprietary ToddTex fabric. Following is a list of these and some other models, including my favorite, the North Face Soloist. The main difference among them is the use of poles—whether or not they use them, and if so, in what configuration. Before buying a bivy, set it up and get inside to see how you feel about the interior.

- Outdoor Research Standard Bivy (1 lb., 4 oz.; no poles)

- Bibler Hooped Bivy (1 lb., 6 oz.; 1 pole)

- Mountain Hardwear Ethereal Bivy (1 lb., 12 oz.; 2 poles)

- Moonstone Nada Tent (1 lb., 15 oz.; 2 poles)

- Outdoor Research Advanced Bivy (1 lb., 15 oz.; 2 poles)

- North Face Soloist Bivy (2 lb., 1 oz.; 2 poles)

- Bibler Tripod Bivy (2 lb., 3 oz.; 3 poles)

CHAPTER 3
SLEEPING BAGS

SLEEPING BAGS HAVE COME A LONG way. The technology of modern bags is astounding, considering that all a sleeping bag is meant to do is keep you warm while you sleep. Reading through the catalogs of companies that sell sleeping bags is like studying a medical textbook: V-channel and trapezoidal baffles, optimized differential cuts, DryLoft composite laminates, and on and on. Do you need to understand all these technical terms to find the right bag for ultralight backpacking? Perhaps if you were writing a doctoral dissertation on them, but otherwise it's all pretty simple.

The basic premise behind sleeping-bag design is to trap warm air that your body generates. The less heat dissipated through the bag and into the open, the warmer you'll be. There is no inherent heat-generating ability to a sleeping bag. The only thing that makes a sleeping bag warm is the body inside it.

Of all the various insulative materials in the world, sleeping-bag makers have nar-rowed their selection to two general categories—synthetics and down—chosen for their low weight, high insulation value, and compressibility. Let's take a look at the pros and cons of each to figure out what works best for ultralight backpacking.

DOWN VERSUS SYNTHETICS

Synthetic-filled sleeping bags use either short-staple fibers (usually Hollofill or Quallofil) or continuous-filament fibers. Continuous-filament is becoming the standard for synthetic bags, with Polarguard being the most popular brand used by bag makers. The newer versions of Polarguard—the 3D and HV—have a hollow core that makes them lighter and more compressible than earlier types.

This is one arena, however, in which the man-made contribution still falls well short of the best all-round natural insulation on the planet: high-quality goose down.

The insulation fill in sleeping bags works

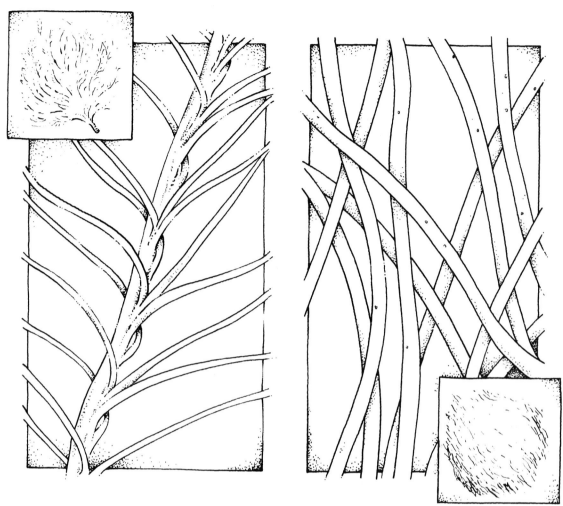

Down (left) versus synthetic (right) fibers.

by trapping tiny pockets of air within its fibers. It is these pockets of air that your body warms up, and the more there are, the warmer you'll be. So far, nothing has come close to down in creating so many thousands of air pockets.

Other advantages of down over the synthetics are numerous, including the two of most interest to the ultralight backpacker: it's lighter in weight and more compressible. By some measures, down can be 35 percent lighter than synthetic fibers giving equal warmth. Down is also softer and can be used across a wider range of temperatures. Down bags last longer than synthetic bags: if you take good care of a down bag, it can serve you well for more than ten years, justifying its higher cost.

I have never owned a synthetic bag, and barring some gigantic leap in technology, I probably never will. The sole disadvantage of down is that it absorbs moisture and therefore loses its insulative properties when wet. Synthetic fibers, on the other hand, are not absorbent; wet synthetics regain their insulative value far more quickly than down. But with the advent of Gore's DryLoft and other water-resistant breathable fabrics and laminates, the problem of wetness no longer needs to apply to down.

We could go on and on with comparing the qualities of down and synthetic fibers, but since this is a book about ultralight backpacking, I'm not going to waste your time. Down wins, hands down.

Now that we've settled that, let's get into detail on how to pick the best bag for your purposes.

THE ULTRALIGHT SLEEPING BAG

Important considerations in selecting a down bag for ultralight backpacking are its loft and fill power. Loft is the natural thickness of a sleeping bag's insulation. Ideally, you want a bag that has the greatest loft that can also be compressed into a small space, and can then return to the original loft when unstuffed.

The industry measures the loft of down by determining its fill power. This is done by taking an ounce of down and putting it in a cylinder, then allowing a lightweight piston to settle on top of the down. The cubic inches of down is then measured, which is its fill power. The highest fill power I have ever seen is 800, which means that after compression

by the piston, an ounce of down takes up 800 cubic inches.

A high fill power indicates two key elements of the down: that it has more air pockets in which to trap your body heat, and that it will more efficiently retain its original loft over the long term. As you might have guessed, along with higher fill power comes higher prices, since the manufacturer has to wait until the goose grows old enough to supply thicker and larger down. And we all know what a hassle it is raising geese past puberty.

The origin of the down sometimes plays a part in its quality as well. European down has generally been of better quality than down from Asia, but this is a minor detail. As long as you stick to fill power that's at least 600, you'll be fine. Of course, if you have the money to spend, go for higher fill power. The greater the fill power, the lighter your bag can be for any particular temperature range.

The way down is arranged in a bag affects how it performs. In a totally hollow sleeping bag, the down would shift all over the place. So bag makers keep the down from shifting by using baffles—tubes that are arranged in a pattern to provide the greatest coverage no matter how much the down has shifted. Most commonly, baffles run across the body, from head to toe.

Modern bags incorporate different strategies to ward off cold spots, which is what you get when the down inside a baffle shifts to one side or another. A common approach is to use slanted baffles; other bags use trapezoidal baffles. Some also have a V-shaped channel running along the sides of the bag so that the down can't shift from the top to the bottom. Any of these designs are sufficient and needn't be given a lot of consideration when choosing your bag.

Temperature Rating

Along with fill power, sleeping bags are advertised by temperature rating. This is a notoriously inaccurate measurement that is supposed to indicate the coldest temperature at which the so-called average person can remain fairly warm inside the bag. Since the temperature rating is generally left up to the manufacturers, they can pretty much plug in any number that seems about right.

These figures make no allowance for whether you are a warm sleeper or a cold sleeper, which can result in a substantial difference. Still, temperature ratings do suggest how warm a bag will be, especially when comparing bags from the same manufacturer. And since there isn't much else to go on in

the showroom for deciding warmth, I'll continue referring to these ratings.

Weight

The weight of a sleeping bag is usually in direct correlation to its temperature rating. The warmest bags are rated −40°F to −60°F and can weigh more than 5 pounds. For the purposes of ultralight backpacking, try to get a bag that weighs 2 pounds or less.

Usually a bag of this weight won't be rated for warmth below 20°F, so you will be somewhat limited as to the conditions you can comfortably encounter. I've used a 15-degree bag in Yosemite in October, when temperatures drop to well below freezing, and slept warmly with nothing more than long underwear on. Your own temperature parameters will play nearly as big a role as your bag in whether you sleep warm or cold.

Zippers

One of the heavier items on a sleeping bag is the zipper, which graces just about every bag out there. A zipper exists purely for convenience at the price of warmth and weight. A draft tube must be inserted along the zipper's length to make up for its lack of insulative value. Sometimes it seems that the zipper is there solely to drive you crazy as it catches on the material every time you use it. The only real advantage I can see to a zipper is that it allows you to join two bags together. Some manufacturers, like Marmot and Moonstone, in an effort to save a little weight, have shortened the zipper so that it only comes down to three-quarters or less of the regular full length. Sierra Designs has eliminated the zipper altogether in their Moonlight bag.

Cut

Every bag is cut differently. Almost all bags use a basic mummy shape, tapering with your body, but widths can vary greatly from bag to bag. Some companies make bags that are gender-specific, pooling more of the down over different sensitive areas and cutting the profile of the bag to more closely fit average measurements for both men and women. The differences are slight. I've never heard of any big problem arising from a woman using a man's bag or vice versa. Beware of any bag that purports to be the lightest in history, but achieves that distinction by being so tight you can't even draw a breath. Test out a bag's cut by getting into it and moving around.

Since your body has to heat the space inside a bag, it makes sense that the smaller the space, the quicker it will heat up. A tighter bag also weighs less and compacts more tightly than a roomier one. You do have to give up a little elbow room for the sake of light weight.

I've found that Marmot and Moonstone bags tend to be cut more generously than other ultralight bags, while those from Western Mountaineering and Feathered Friends are among the tightest.

Water Resistance

DryLoft, PTFE, and other similar water-resistant breathable materials provide a way to combat the greatest disadvantage of down. Once down gets wet, it loses almost all its loft and hence all those air pockets, and it becomes next to useless in preserving warmth. The ingenious people at the W. L. Gore company invented a water-resistant and highly breathable laminate that can be added to sleeping bag shells. You can literally take a cup of water and pour it onto a bag that has a DryLoft shell and watch the water bead off without a single drop being absorbed into the material. DryLoft is also windproof, which helps keep the inside of the bag toasty warm.

Compared with Gore-Tex, DryLoft is not quite as waterproof, but it is much more breathable. DryLoft bags weigh a little bit more, and they have a strange crunchy texture to them, which can make stuffing quite a chore (tip: turn the bag inside out before stuffing). DryLoft bags are great if you'll be traveling in an extremely wet or damp environment, but I've never found them to be all that necessary in other climates.

An alternative to DryLoft is a microfiber

fabric, such as that used in some Western Mountaineering bags. The shell is made of a polyester fabric with an extremely high thread count—so high, in fact, that water has a difficult time squeezing through the spaces between the threads. Yet it is still very breathable and light, and makes for a good choice in wet conditions without paying the cost of DryLoft in money and weight. Since the water-repellency is built right into the fabric, it will last as long as the bag.

Some Ultralight Sleeping Bags

My own ultralight sleeping bag is a Western Mountaineering UltraLite. Here are its specifications, as well as those of some other recommended models that have been available (the figure in inches refers to torso girth).

- Marmot Hydrogen (1 lb., 7 oz.; 775 fill; 30°F; 62 in.)

- Sierra Designs Moonlight (1 lb., 7 oz.; 600 fill; 30°F; 60 in.)

- Feathered Friends Hummingbird PTFE (1 lb., 10 oz.; 800+ fill; 20°F; 58 in.)

- Western Mountaineering UltraLite (1 lb., 12 oz.; 750+ fill; 25°F; 59 in.)

- Moonstone Ultralight (1 lb., 12 oz., 800 fill; 25°F; 62 in.)

If you backpack only in warm climates, you can use a bag that weighs as little as 14 ounces, such as the Western Mountaineering LineLite. Another interesting option is the Feathered Friends Rock Wren, which has a half-length zipper in the front, zippered arm holes, and a drawstringed hole at the bottom. This way, the bag does double duty as an overcoat of sorts, which you can wear around the campsite (at least until people start making fun of you).

As you shop for a bag, try to get the measurements on how small a sack it can be stuffed into. Whether or not you actually use a stuff sack on your trips, this will give you an idea of how tightly the bag can be

The Marmot Hydrogen.
Courtesy Marmot

compressed. My Western Mountaineering bag, for example, can be stuffed into a sack 7 by 13 inches. If these figures aren't available, at least shove the bag into the stuff sack that comes with it to get an idea of how compact it is. Even better is to have your ultralight backpack with you so you can check on how well the compressed sleeping bag fits into the bottom of the pack.

Duvet-Style Bags

In an effort to save weight, some companies offer bags that cover only your sides and top—like a comforter—and count on the sleeping pad to insulate the bottom. I'm not entirely convinced I can stay warm enough in such a bag since there will inevitably be some leakage along the sides. It's also less comfortable, since you lose the padding of the

down beneath you. And if you're a shifty sleeper, the bag can come loose and release the heat that your body has worked so hard to generate.

The GoLite bag has a three-quarter wrap design and uses Velcro tabs along the side to secure it to the sleeping pad. The 20-degree Fur system from GoLite, which includes the bag and sleeping pad, weighs 3 pounds, 3 ounces.

CARE OF YOUR BAG

When you set up camp, unstuff your sleeping bag as soon as you can. The less time a bag spends stuffed up, the longer it will retain its loft. I always get my sleeping system set up as soon as I reach my campsite.

If your bag gets wet during the night, dry

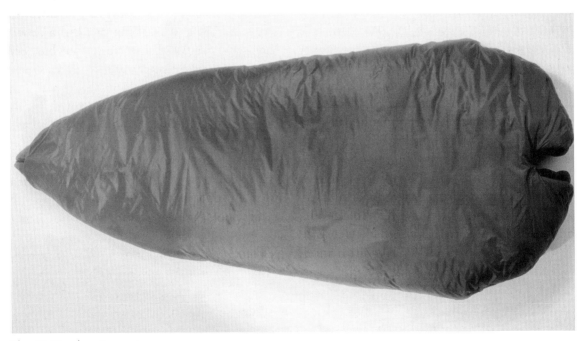

The GoLite sleeping system. Courtesy GoLite

THE ULTRALIGHT WAY: BE A BAG-WARMER

A sleeping bag works only if something inside of it is generating heat. Therefore you want to try to get yourself as warm as possible before crawling inside.

Steps you can take before getting into the bag include exercising (jumping jacks work well), eating (the warmer the food, the better), and emptying your bladder. Omitting this last activity can have a chilling effect on your heat-generating ability, since your body expends heat to keep the fluid inside your bladder warm (and don't forget what a hassle it is to stumble outside in the middle of the night to relieve yourself).

You can put some of your clothes inside the bag to create more insulation, with the added benefit of providing you with warm clothes in the morning. Finally, bear in mind that 85 percent of your body heat can be lost through your head, so be sure to wear a warm hat during the night. By using these techniques, you can stay comfortable in a lighter-weight, higher-temperature-rated bag than you might otherwise need.

it as much as you can the next morning before packing everything up, providing conditions are dry. Turn the bag inside out, assuming the inside is darker in color than the exterior, because darker colors will absorb more of the sun's heat. Even if the bag doesn't seem to be wet, let it hang out until you're ready to pack up and move out. It might not feel wet to the touch, but a bag's fill can become damp from sweat. To prevent buildup of excess moisture, cinch up the draft collar and keep your head out of the bag at night so that you're not exhaling your moisture-laden breath into it.

If you need to hit the trail as soon as you leave the night's slumber behind, you can lash the sleeping bag to the top of your pack and let it dry as you walk (see photo, page 44).

When the Trip Is Over

After you return home, store your bag by hanging it from the foot, with the zipper open, so the bag can air out and also maintain the integrity of its loft. During your trips, try to keep the bag clean enough so you don't need to launder it. Down bags hold the same opinion of the laundry as dogs do of the vet. A bad washing can kill a down bag, so if you do need to clean your bag, try to get it done professionally—and I don't mean any old dry cleaner. Go to a place with specific resources for washing down bags.

If you would rather wash a bag at home, here's how to do it: First, make sure you use only soap designed for washing down, such as Down Suds. Fill a bathtub halfway with warm water and a small amount of soap and dunk the bag right in. Using a squeezing motion with your hands, work your way up and down the bag until it is thoroughly saturated. Drain the water and turn on the shower to rinse the bag, using the same squeezing motion until all the soap has washed out. Turn off the shower and squeeze out as much excess water as you can before

If your bag is wet in the morning and it's not raining, secure the bag to your pack when you hike out of camp to let it dry.

carrying the soggy bundle in a large towel to the dryer. Don't try to pick it up with just your hands, because when the bag is soaked the baffles inside can rip from the weight of the wet down. Use low heat in the dryer, and throw in a couple of tennis balls to prevent the down from clumping.

Be aware that no matter how much care is taken in washing a down bag, it will inevitably lose some of its loft each time. I used to work at a backpacking store that rented both down and synthetic sleeping bags, which would be washed after every rental. A year after the bags were brand-new and had gone through countless washings, a 20-degree synthetic bag had more insulative value than a 0-degree down bag. Call me what you will, but I've owned my current

down bag for four years and haven't washed it yet.

Once you've used a down bag on several trips, it may lose some of its loft from continual stuffing and unstuffing. To regain some of the loft, throw the bag into a tumble dryer set to low heat. This process does wonders to fluff up and reinvigorate lethargic down. Just be sure to check the bag every few minutes for hot spots, which are prone to melting if left in too long.

SLEEPING PADS

People new to backpacking sometimes resent giving up their luxurious bedroom mattress for a piece of 1-inch-thick foam. To help people make this transition, Cascade Designs came up with its Therm-a-Rest pad. This is an open-cell foam pad sandwiched between an outer layer of waterproof polyurethane that self-inflates when you roll it out and open a nozzle. When it's inflated, screw down the nozzle and, presto, a cushy mattress is yours. When it's time to break camp, unscrew the nozzle and roll up the pad, squeezing out all the air.

To be honest, I don't have a particularly high opinion of the Therm-a-Rest. The ones I've owned developed leaks within a couple months, rendering them unusable. Once, the puncture happened on the first night of a five-day trip, so I had the dubious pleasure of having only the bottom of my sleeping bag for insulation and comfort while lugging around more than a pound of useless foam.

The possibility of something like that happening again has made me a staunch supporter of the "simpler is always, always better" philosophy. Therefore I usually use Cascade Designs' leaner offering, the Ridge Rest. This is a waterproof, closed-cell foam pad that has ridges running across it from top to bottom, which trap warm air in addition to providing a little extra thickness. It weighs half as much as a Therm-a-Rest, and very little can go wrong with it. Plus, there's no hassle with having to blow it up or, later, working to get all the air out.

Ridge Rests are 20 inches wide, 72 inches long, and ⁵/₈-inch thick. I lop off about a third of the pad to save weight and bulk, so that it extends from my neck to mid-thigh. When I use it, I can hardly tell that there's no pad below this point. If the ground is rocky or cold, I put extra clothes under my lower legs.

There are, however, reasons why a Therm-a-Rest might be the better choice for you. The problem with closed-cell foam such as that used in the Ridge Rest is that it doesn't compress, so you're stuck with a big, fat roll that you have to lash to your pack. A Therm-a-Rest can be folded and placed compactly against the inside of your pack. You might even be able to use it to replace the padding that came with the pack. For example, some of the Osprey Aether packs include a foam pad that slides into a pocket between your back and the inside of the pack. You can easily slide this pad out and use a folded-up Therm-a-Rest instead, somewhat offsetting its heavier weight.

Therm-a-Rests come in many lengths, widths, and thicknesses. The only version I would recommend is the UltraLite, which weighs 1 pound, measures 20 by 47 inches, and is 1 inch thick.

If your choice in sleeping pads comes down to which type is more affordable, the simpler closed-cell-foam model wins easily.

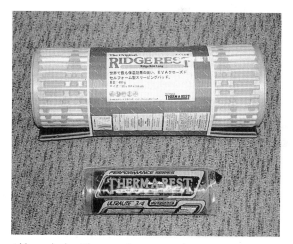

Although the Therm-a-Rest is much more compact than the Ridge Rest, it's almost twice as heavy.

Either way, your backpacking mattress is going to be a far cry from your mattress back home. No matter what you end up with, it will take some getting used to.

TRIMMING THE FAT

Other than cutting off the odd tassel or tag, there really isn't much you can do to trim fat from your sleeping bag. As long as you get yourself the lightest, most compressible bag that you're confident will keep you warm at night, you can rest easy.

If you decide to use a closed-cell foam sleeping pad, such as the Ridge Rest, you can save some weight by trimming the sides and ends. Do this only if you're not a person who squirms around a lot at night. I find myself rolling off the pad, so I leave the edges intact.

Eventually you may find that on certain trips where the temperature is warm and the ground soft, you don't need a sleeping pad at all. I've done this a few times with no major complaints. And as any ultralight backpacker will tell you, every ounce left at home is an ounce that you don't have to carry.

CHAPTER 4
FOOTWEAR

ONE HOT SUMMER DAY IN THE Colorado Rockies, I parked my truck at the trailhead and strapped on my pack. It was my first solo backpacking trip, and I couldn't wait to hike up the trail and find an idyllic spot to camp among the pine trees and crystal-clear lakes. This was before I discovered ultralight backpacking. I laced up my heavy leather boots and started walking, the 40-pound pack biting into my shoulders.

Everything felt pretty good until I reached the first major uphill push. I had been expecting the 2,000-foot climb, so I dug in and slowly made my way up the trail. About halfway to the top my feet started feeling a little sore. I ignored it and kept climbing. By the time I reached the crest of the trail, my feet were aching like a high-schooler's heart on Valentine's Day. Later that afternoon, I set up camp and gently took off my shoes to inspect the damage. It wasn't pretty. Oozing blisters had formed in several places, and even a light touch on any part of my foot felt like a pounding hammer. I couldn't

understand why this was happening. I had spent weeks breaking in the stiff boots by wearing them around town, and everyone told me they were a good brand.

The next morning, I reluctantly stepped back into my boots and began the return hike to the trailhead. I had planned to stay out a day longer, but all I could think about was getting home and letting a warm bath soak the pain away. I lumbered down the trail, wincing with every step. By the time I made it all the way back, I was ready to give up backpacking forever.

Once I calmed down and my feet returned to normal, I set about looking for a better way. There were already a few people out there hiking in plain old tennis shoes or sneakers, and they were raving about their comfort. This seemed a little drastic at the time, but it sounded a lot better than those monstrous boots.

I got a pair of lightweight trail shoes and, not without a healthy measure of trepidation, set off on another backpacking trip.

The difference was unbelievable. No blisters, no soreness, no pain. I felt like I was walking twice as fast, even though my pack weighed about the same. I had become a believer. On the Pacific Crest Trail, I wore the same trail shoes (but with a much lighter pack) and walked 20-mile days without getting even a single blister.

THE BIG SWITCH

The switch from traditional backpacking boots to lightweight trail shoes offers perhaps the most sweeping benefit of all the changes you can make in becoming an ultralight backpacker. The difference it makes in a backpacking experience is truly astounding. I still see people out on the trail, heaving up a mountain with those concrete blocks on their feet, and I wonder why they haven't switched.

It's interesting to note that there are proportionally more people traveling in lightweight trail shoes on long-distance thru-hikes (such as the Appalachian Trail) than on weekend backpacking trips. A traditional backpacker might counter that these thru-hikers are much more fit and can therefore withstand the added rigors of hiking in trail shoes. But you'd be surprised how many unfit people successfully tackle the nation's long-distance trails in lightweight footwear. And if thru-hikers are walking 20 miles and more each day in lightweight shoes, then surely weekend backpackers can hike 5 or 10 miles in them.

The use of lightweight shoes hinges on the premise that you'll be using other techniques of ultralight backpacking to keep your pack-weight to a minimum. The shoes are just a part of the overall ultralight program.

THE NAKED FOOT

Of the two million years that humans have been roaming the planet, only a few thousand have found us wearing shoes. The structure of the foot is the result of eons of evolutionary adaptation, almost all built on the premise that we walk with naked feet. The naked foot is an amazing piece of machinery that is primarily designed to support our weight and propel us forward. It contains 26 bones, 38 muscles, and 126 ligaments, making it the most complicated part of the musculoskeletal system. To make full use of the foot's ability to handle our weight and move us around, we would ideally need to keep it naked and unshod. Only then can it work in a completely natural state.

Now, however, we have become so accustomed to wearing shoes that walking around with nothing on our feet seems almost unnatural. Shoes have become a kind of handicap that restricts the natural movements of all those bones and muscles. We now consider some kind of added support a necessity. Indeed, a shoe's sole protects our feet from rough ground, while a frame for the heel and arch helps support the leg and the rest of the body. But because the design of our feet was born from so many millennia of walking and running with no extra support at all, we ideally want to retain the natural movement of the foot as much as possible. The less restrictive the shoe, the freer the foot is to perform as it has been designed to do.

The naked foot has the distinctive ability to contour around uneven ground. The bones are structured so that the foot tries to make even contact with the ground all along its length. This gives it the added leverage it needs to propel our bodies in a certain direction. To illustrate this concept, put your

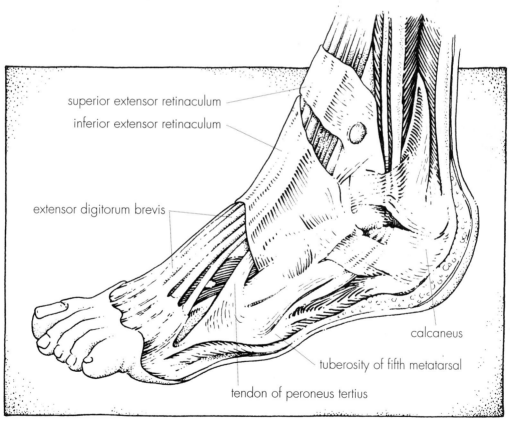

superior extensor retinaculum

inferior extensor retinaculum

extensor digitorum brevis

calcaneus

tuberosity of fifth metatarsal

tendon of peroneus tertius

Musculoskeletal structure of the foot.

fingertips against a wall and push your body away; you'll see that you won't move as far and as fast as you would if you put your whole hands flat on the wall.

Because shoe soles are stiffer than our feet, the foot can't conform as well to the ground beneath, so some force is lost as we push forward. It gets even worse when the sole is as hard as those found on traditional backpacking boots. The single purpose of a sole is to prevent stones, roots, and other obstructions from digging into our feet. Unless you're walking on metal spikes, the sole of almost any lightweight shoe does this job quite well.

The foot also performs well at keeping us balanced. The muscles of our feet are constantly adjusting and readjusting to keep our weight and momentum balanced. If you stand on one foot, you can feel the different muscles flexing and relaxing to keep you upright. As you walk, these muscles have a harder time keeping you in balance when they are encased in a solid structure. I found that my balance on the trail improved greatly when I switched to lightweight footwear.

Lighter weight is much easier on the plantar fascia, the vital connective tissue that runs from heel to toe at the bottom of each foot. In addition, the other ligaments, tendons, and muscles of the body will breathe a sigh of relief when they aren't supporting a great deal of weight.

ANKLE SUPPORT

Many people argue that the load a backpack places upon the lower leg and foot demands the protection of a thick, stiff, cast-like boot.

But the argument is based on the assumption that the pack weighs upward of 50 pounds. With a pack that weighs less than half that much, the weight borne by the ankle and foot becomes almost negligible. I have heard of far more foot-related injuries resulting from wearing traditional boots than from wearing lightweight trail shoes. As long-distance hiker Chris Townsend says in *The Backpacker's Handbook* (Ragged Mountain Press): "Footwear should also provide *support* for your foot and ankle, though this is less important than some people think. . . . some running shoes give more ankle support than some boots do."

Boot manufacturers often want you to believe that you need a large, heavily padded boot to protect your foot. This is simply a reflection of the consumers who fear that hiking in trail shoes is foolhardy. It's time to bring such fears in line with reality.

A common misconception is that ankle support comes primarily from the height of the boot extending over and above the ankle. When I worked as a boot fitter for a specialty outdoor shop, I was amazed at how deeply this belief ran. As a response, I would take a boot off the wall and bend the top part of the boot back and forth to show there was no way that significant support can come from this part of the shoe. Even after providing literature on the subject and relating my personal experiences, some people simply could not be convinced that ankle support has practically nothing to do with the height of the shoe. Ankle support comes almost entirely from how stable a shoe keeps your arch and heel (see the section on insoles, beginning on page 57).

Of course, ultralight backpacking requires

common sense. If you're going on an expedition to Denali or hiking Mount Whitney's East Face in January, traditional boots are a prudent choice. If you have weak ankles or have had ankle surgery in the past, stiffer boots may be a better option, although after breaking my own ankle I was back on the trail hiking in lightweight shoes within four months. If you are hiking in extremely rugged conditions, such as a multiday hike over talus, you'll want the extra stability of boots. But these are all special circumstances that don't negate the general rule that hiking in lightweight trail shoes is easier and safer—and ultimately more enjoyable.

THE ULTRALIGHT SHOE

There is an overwhelming choice of models when it comes to footwear, but the only criteria you really need to be concerned with are weight and comfort. Many backpacking books inundate you with unneeded footwear information about full-grain one-piece leather uppers, molded polyurethane midsoles, combination lasting, and so on. I've seen expert backpackers hike in everything from 20-dollar department-store sneakers to sandals to top-of-the-line trail-running shoes, and most don't know the difference between a heel counter and a toe box.

So rather than describe every little detail of a shoe's various components, let's concentrate on how to find a trail shoe that's comfortable and appropriate for ultralight backpacking. After all, when you're out on the trail, it doesn't matter one bit whether your footwear was made with a Norwegian welt or a Littleway welt, as long as it's comfortable and stays comfortable.

When you first walk into a shoe store and see the endless array of boots that are available, you might want to turn around and walk right out again. But you can eliminate many of the selections that are in the traditional boot category, making the choices a little less overwhelming. First, look for simplicity. If a trail shoe is blazing with all sorts

Bend the toe and heel together to see how much the shoe flexes. The toe should bend beyond ninety degrees.

of neon colors and has some space-age design for tying the laces, you can bet that the manufacturer is trying to sell the product on looks alone.

Try to shop for shoes in the afternoon or evening, after your feet have swelled due to the day's activities. You will be able to fit your shoes more accurately, because hiking causes your feet to swell considerably larger than your regular size. I can't tell you how many times I've seen someone buy a pair of shoes that fit like a dream in the morning and then end up with blackened toenails from a hike. Well-fitting hiking shoes should be about a half-size to a size bigger than your normal size, and even more if your daily dis-

tance increases—up to a size and a half larger for a long-distance hiker.

Weight and Flex

Pick up the shoes to test them for a rough weight. Hold a different model of shoe in each hand to see which is lightest. Start with the lightest shoe on the wall and work your way up.

Another test is to hold the shoe at the heel and the toe and bend it to see how stiff the sole is. You should be able to curl the toe right up past vertical. Usually the middle of the shoe is stiffer than the toe and heel, which is acceptable as long as it flexes at least a little bit. If any part of the sole remains completely rigid, move on to the next shoe.

The Sole

Turn the shoe upside down and inspect the sole. Look for a sole that has grooves at least a quarter of an inch wide so that it can grip the ground better. Thinner grooves will still work, but will be more prone to sliding off the terrain. The grooves should not be too deep, since you want as much of the sole to make contact with the ground as possible, while still retaining some degree of traction.

Seams

Check to see how many different pieces of material are used to make the shoe. Seams running all over the shoe create two problems. One is that the shoe has more chances to fall apart, since a seam is the first place that will succumb to the ravages of the trail. The second problem offers the more compelling reason to get a shoe with few seams: blisters. Because a seam brings two pieces of material together, it is more likely to rub against your foot than a smooth, uninterrupted surface.

Trying on the Shoes

Try on each pair of shoes you are interested in and spend some time walking around the store to see how they feel. Wear the same kind of socks you'll have on when you hike. The store may have a small ramp that you can use to test how well the shoes grip and flex. As you walk up, lift your heels to see if they slide inside the shoe—up to half an inch is acceptable. When you walk down, the shoe should hold your foot in a stable position so that your toes don't ram up against the front of the shoe. The toe box should be roomy enough so that you can wiggle your toes, since this will allow your feet to swell unimpeded.

Check for adequate cushioning around your foot and for any part of the shoe that could dig into your skin. One way to do this is to hold onto something for balance and take a very slow, deep step, concentrating on any anomalies in the shoe. One pair that I tried were no good because the laces, when tied, came too high up the tongue and dug into the top of my foot. As you try each pair of shoes, employ the "guilty until proven innocent" approach. Assume the shoe has some flaws; your job is to find them.

One way to test shoes thoroughly before buying is to bring your loaded backpack to the store with you. This way, you can test the shoes under more realistic conditions. Don't be afraid to take your sweet time trying on different shoes and walking around with your pack on. Selecting the right shoe is a crucial decision, so don't feel pressured to change into the next pair after five minutes.

Once you find a pair that seems to work well for you, make a list of the other pairs that you tried on. Again, make sure you can return the shoes you are buying in case they prove to be uncomfortable. Because lightweight trail shoes don't have to be broken in like leather boots, you can start hiking in them with a loaded pack as soon as you wish. Pick a trail that has both ups and downs and varied terrain, and hike for at least 8 miles. That should give you a pretty good idea of how the shoe fits.

My Montrail Vitesses, after about 800 miles.

Some Ultralight Shoes

Here are a few recommendations for appropriate ultralight shoes. Remember, everyone's foot is different, so just because your friend said her Vitesses are perfect doesn't mean they are going to fit your feet as well. This listing includes the weight for each pair of shoes in a size 9 for men and size 7 for women.

- Montrail Vitesse: men's 1 lb., 8 oz.; women's 1 lb., 4 oz.

- Montrail Hurricane Ridge GTX (Gore-Tex): men's 1 lb., 8 oz.; women's 1 lb., 4 oz.

- Merrell Terrator: men's 1 lb., 10 oz.; women's 1 lb., 6 oz.

- Garmont Aroya: men's 1 lb., 15 oz.; women's 1 lb., 11 oz.

- North Face Avalanche Creek Low (Gore-Tex): men's 1 lb., 15 oz.; women's 1 lb., 11 oz.

- Lowa Tempest Low: men's 2 lb.; women's 1 lb., 13 oz.

Sandals

Many backpackers are finding benefits in wearing sandals. They offer much better ventilation than anything else, you don't need to wear socks, and you can wade through streams without dealing with wet shoes. However, sandals do need specific circumstances to work well: a warm and sunny day, a relatively flat trail that's clear of toe-stubbing obstacles, and relatively shorter distances. If you're expecting anything other than these ideal conditions, you'll have to bring along regular hiking shoes as well. Since sandals can weigh over a pound, you're better off leaving them at home.

Another drawback to sandals is that they apply pressure along the straps, creating an ideal environment for blisters. If you have tough, callused feet or make a living as a firewalker, this might not be much of a problem. But for the rest of us, regular trail shoes do a much better job of keeping the dreaded blister at bay.

TRIMMING THE FAT

When you've finally decided on the pair of shoes that's just right for you, it's time for those scissors again.

Cut off any extra lace material, making sure to burn the new ends to prevent fray-

Some ultralight backpackers hike in sandals, with varying degrees of success.

ing. Also, many shoes have fabric loops to tug on as a way to help you get into them. You shouldn't have any problem doing away with these and anything else that looks like it doesn't serve a necessary purpose.

RAIN AND WETNESS

One of the obvious drawbacks to lightweight trail shoes is that they generally aren't water-resistant (though the incorporation of waterproof-breathable materials is beginning to change this). Traditional backpackers regularly point out this limitation when trying to demonstrate the inferiority of the shoes

compared with leather boots. Indeed, this is one argument that doesn't have a powerful comeback, but the problem of zero water-resistance isn't as bad as it might seem.

The first reply you could give to the traditional backpacker is this: "Well, your big old boots aren't all that water-resistant either." Leather is not impervious to water. If you stand in 4 inches of water in leather boots, your socks and feet will eventually get wet. Owners of leather boots must apply and reapply water-resistant wax or sealant to aid in repelling water.

Many boot manufacturers have introduced models that incorporate a Gore-Tex membrane sandwiched between layers of the boot, but so far only a few ultralight shoes include this waterproof-breathable component. I hope that more shoe makers integrate it into their lightweight footwear. The Montrail Hurricane Ridge GTX is a good ultralight shoe that uses Gore-Tex. It weighs no more than the Montrail Vitesse but is fully waterproof.

If it looks like there will be a lot of rain on a trip, you can bring along a pair of gaiters to cover the gap between your pant legs and shoes. The idea is not so much to make your feet more comfortable as it is to avoid excess water in your socks and shoes that would add to the weight you're carrying. Of course, gaiters weigh something too. I've used gaiters only once, and they weren't an appreciable improvement.

SHOE CARE

Many traditional backpackers argue that lightweight shoes don't last as long as leather

To be honest, the best solution if you are wearing lightweight trail shoes that don't resist water is to just accept that your feet are wet and not make a big deal out of it.

I've hiked plenty of times with wet feet and I've come to not mind it much at all. Toward the beginning of a two-week trip along the Pacific Crest Trail, it rained continuously for several days. My feet were soaked from the time I stepped out of the tent to the time I turned in for the night. Once I accepted that my feet were going to be wet and there was nothing I could do about it, I hardly noticed the squish-squish of every step.

I'd be lying if I said I enjoyed every soggy step of that hike, but I was certainly a lot happier than I would be stomping around in big leather boots—which eventually would have become just as soaked. The advantage of trail shoes over boots when both are wet is that the former will dry much more quickly. And increasingly, ultralight backpackers have the option of footwear that incorporates waterproof-breathable materials.

---

boots. I've put more than a thousand rough trail miles on my Montrail Vitesses, and not a single stitch has come undone. Even if leather boots do last longer than lightweight trail shoes, the argument makes as much sense as saying that a regular car doesn't last as long as a tank. It may be true, but if you don't abuse either one, they will both last a long, long time. And, as with a tank, boots cost considerably more than their lightweight alternative.

There isn't much you need to do to care for a lightweight trail shoe. Traditional boots require a lot more attention to keep them supple and water-resistant. Since most ultralight shoes aren't meant to be water-resistant in the first place, you don't have to bother with sealants and waxes. If you come home with very dirty shoes, it's a good idea to hose off the mud and dirt, but that's really about it. I do like to inspect my shoes between each trip to be sure the seams are all in place, there aren't any cracks or tears,

the sole is intact, and the laces are in good condition.

There will come a time, however, when the shoe naturally begins to break down. You might not even notice anything by looking at it, because much of the deterioration is internal. Every thousand trail miles is a good time to buy a new pair of shoes. Assuming you hike fairly regularly, this works out to between three and five years. If you go backpacking only once every two months or so, your shoes could last much longer. However, depending on the particular shoes you buy and how well made they are, you might have to replace them more often.

A good way to tell if you need new shoes (other than obvious signs of deterioration) is to try on a new pair of exactly the same model and see how much difference there is between the two. If the difference is drastic, consider replacing your pair. If you find yourself becoming quite attached to your hiking shoes, there's no reason to switch to a different model. As long as the manufacturer continues making the model of shoe that I wear, I'll continue buying the same one.

INSOLES

The insole of the shoe might be the first thing to give way to the ravages of time. Many people favor the use of custom insoles, which fit your foot better and last longer. Such insoles are created using a vacuum process to make an impression of your feet onto an insole. I've used custom insoles in my ski boots, where an even pressure along the length of the boot is vital, but I've never used these hardened, customized insoles in hiking shoes.

However, I've been won over by mass-produced, semicustom insoles. I use the Superfeet brand, which employs a hardened

plastic shell beneath the heel and arch, and a comfortable foam material for the insole itself. These insoles aren't fully customized, since the shape is fixed at the factory, but the extra support they provide is invaluable.

Since ankle support depends on how stable the shoe keeps your arch and heel, Superfeet and other such replacement insoles provide a tremendous amount of extra support without adding weight or bulk. Not only do they partially correct for pronation (inward rolling of the foot) and supination (outward rolling), but they also help to prevent your foot bones from elongating with every step. The result is feet that are much less fatigued at the end of the day, and fewer foot problems over the long term. To use these insoles, simply find the appropriate size in the store's display. Then take out the flimsy insoles that come with the shoe and replace them with

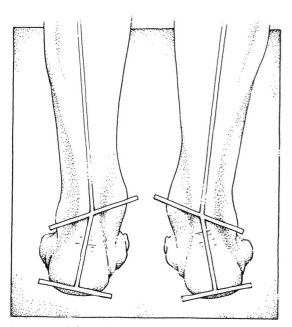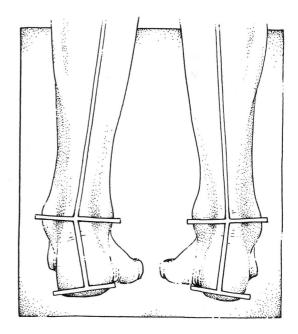

Pronation (left) and supination (right).

the semicustom model. I highly recommend these in any shoe.

Some people's skeletal structure might necessitate the use of greater support than that offered by the mass-produced insoles. If your feet pronate or supinate excessively, fully customized insoles might help to alleviate the problem. An easy way to tell if this is the case is to stand with your bare feet shoulder-width apart on flat ground and have someone stand behind you. If they notice an obvious tilt to your ankles and feet either to the inside or the outside—or if you already know you have alignment problems—then consult a podiatrist or a knowledgeable fitter of customized insoles.

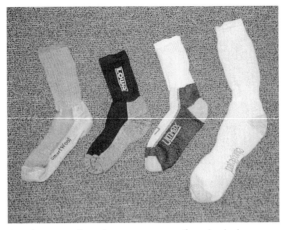

A selection of socks appropriate for ultralight backpacking.

SOCKS

Choosing the right pair of socks shouldn't be too hard. Practically any pair on the wall of a camping store that displays itself as a hiking sock is fine. Look for socks that have a thin to medium thickness. You definitely don't need expedition socks; the light hiking versions are ideal. I have always been satisfied with Thorlo-Padd hiking and trekking socks. Among other brands that offer well-made socks are Wigwam and SmartWool.

Some people swear by socks made at least partially of wool. My only criteria for a good pair of socks is that they fit well and are comfortable, don't bunch up, aren't too thick,

and won't become totally soaked with sweat or too hot on a sunny summer day. There are many socks out there that don't use any wool but meet my needs just fine. Spend your time and energy on shoes; don't worry too much about the socks. If you want wool, get ones that use merino wool (SmartWool and Wigwam are among the brands that offer socks that use merino and are extremely comfortable). Don't ever wear cotton socks, which get wet easily and stay wet.

Because you won't be carrying a heavy pack, your feet won't sweat as much. And since your ultralight shoes are far more breathable than a traditional backpacking boot, your sweat can evaporate much more easily. Hence there's no need for sock liners. One pair of socks on your feet is just fine.

CHAPTER 5
CLOTHING

WE'VE SEEN IN PREVIOUS CHAPTERS that there are abundant choices in gear for ultralight backpacking. Yet options for clothing outnumber all the gear choices combined. Step into any retail outdoors store and prepare for sensory overload as you take in the racks and racks of clothing of every conceivable shape, color, fabric, and style. Even when you limit your view to just the items appropriate for going ultralight, the selection is daunting.

There's nothing wrong with such a glut of choices, since it gives us a huge selection from which to choose our ideal clothing. We just need to know what we're getting, why we're getting it, and how to use it once we have it. We've accomplished this task with backpacks, shelter, sleeping bags, and footwear, and now we'll do the same with clothing.

Clothing really only serves a handful of important purposes. Despite what some promoters might have you believe, no clothing bestows superpowers that enable you to leap tall mountains in a single bound. Very simply, the principal purpose of clothing is to insulate your body so that it maintains a normal, healthy temperature. Clothing does that by creating a barrier that reduces the impact of the environment upon the sensitive internal temperature controls of the body and by trapping the heat that the body generates.

In the temperature-controlled world of the home or office, clothing doesn't serve much more of a purpose than social modesty and style. But nature has a mind of its own, and the clothing we use in the wilderness must be made to a much higher standard. In the brutal cold of winter in Alaska, for example, we need clothing that can insulate our bodies so that no precious heat escapes. Meanwhile, in the blistering, brutal heat of summer in the Sahara, our needs are for clothing that shelters us from the sun while keeping our skin cool and dry.

As ultralight backpackers, we also need clothing that's as light and compactable as possible. For clothing to qualify as ultralight, it must be very lightweight and easily com-

Selecting the right clothing can be overwhelming given the vast ocean of choices.

pressed without sacrificing comfort and performance. Fortunately for the ultralight backpacker, manufacturers are constantly introducing new garments that offer the same performance as outdated products but weigh less and take up less space.

Let me say at this point that no matter what clothing materials you decide to use for your trips, please don't ever wear cotton in any form. Its inherent properties are exactly the opposite of what we need from a material: it gets wet easily, remains wet forever, becomes heavy when wet, and is our body's sworn enemy. Cotton bad, very bad.

THE LAYERING SYSTEM

Amazingly, there is clothing that can meet all our outdoors requirements admirably. This clothing is best used as part of a system in which different kinds of garments are worn in layers to protect the body's core temperature. The most practical and common system involves three layers: the inner layer keeps you dry, the middle layer keeps you warm, and the outer layer keeps you both warm and dry. Each layer uses a different strategy to accomplish its task.

Inner Layer

The inner layer of clothing is the most important, because it lies right next to your skin. If the inner layer is not working properly, the whole system collapses. You don't want to run into a store and just pick up anything that looks like long underwear; it's crucial that you get the right inner-layer garment for what you'll be doing.

Good backpacking underwear primarily serves you by keeping your skin dry. Dry skin enables the body to use its natural temperature-controlling mechanisms efficiently. When you become too hot, your body compensates by sweating, which in turn cools your skin through evaporation. If the sweat can't evaporate, it fails to cool the skin. And it blocks any more sweat from coming through the sweat glands.

The underwear we're interested in uses polyester, which is a naturally water-hating (hydrophobic) fiber, the outside of which has been treated with a water-loving (hydrophilic) chemical. In this way, sweat can pass through the weave of the fiber and reach the outside of the material, where it spreads and evaporates.

This method of channeling your sweat through the fabric and dispersing it on the outside is known as wicking, and it is the method of choice for most underwear on the market. Patagonia's Capilene has long been the standard-bearer for wicking fabrics, and is still the most popular. Other companies' fabrics, like Mountain Hardwear's ZeO2, Marmot's DriClime, and the North Face's Micronamics, work similarly and with equally good results.

A variety of other materials are used to make underwear—wool, polypropylene, silk, Thermax—but I've found that nothing works better than treated polyester, like Capilene. It has always kept me dry, even in damp conditions while hiking vigorously, and I've owned the same set of undershirt and long underwear for years. Polyester is practically incapable of absorbing moisture, so it does a fantastic job of insulating your body even when wet. However, because its fibers won't hold water, it can be difficult to remove stains and smells, and these garments sometimes tend to stink after prolonged heavy use. Increasingly, manufacturers are treating this underwear with an odor-eating chemical that leaves the garment smelling rosy-fresh even after a long, sweaty trip.

The only other material I would consider is silk because it is the lightest that can be used for underwear. It absorbs water but maintains its insulating abilities and is an effective wicker, even without special chemical applications. And best of all, it feels wonderful next to the skin. It does, however, take a longer time to dry than Capilene. Terramar's ThermaSilk is a popular brand.

Underwear tops should fit snugly without impeding your ability to breathe and move around comfortably. The closer the material is to your skin, the better it works, so avoid tops that are baggy or loose. Tops come in different styles, some incorporating zippers at the neck. A poorly placed zipper can dig into your skin if you dip your head, and zippers mean extra weight. So find a top without one.

Underwear bottoms should have a tighter fit than tops. A comfortable, tight fit around your legs prevents the garment from drooping as you walk and creates the ideal microclimate for your skin to remain dry. Also, a close fit will allow your body heat to dry the underwear more quickly if it ever gets wet.

Middle Layer (Torso)

Now that we've taken care of keeping you dry, the next step is finding something to keep you warm. For many years synthetic fleece has been the favorite material for keeping folks toasty warm while pursuing activities in the outdoors. Modern advances have breathed new life into good old fleece, and ultralight backpackers have benefited the most. Synthetic fleece is light, warm, comfortable, performs well when wet, and dries quickly. Its disadvantages are lack of wind resistance and low compressibility, and it is exactly these two issues that modern fleece has tried to address.

Let's look at how manufacturers have tackled the problem of staying warm in stiff winds. The body can lose vast amounts of heat to wind and must be protected from it. The only solution used to be a windproof shell worn over your other clothes. A new solution has come in the form of a windproof membrane that is sandwiched between the inner and outer layers of a fleece garment.

The most popular brand is Gore's Windstopper, which can be found in Mountain Hardwear and Marmot clothing; Patagonia's version is called *PEF*. Windbloc, by Malden Mills (makers of Polartec), is yet another rendition. Not only do all of these repel wind, but they also remain almost as breathable as regular fleece, so you're not sweating like an overworked mule while wearing garments that use them. The fleece garments that use a windproof membrane can also be effectively worn as an outer shell, although they aren't waterproof so you still need something for when it rains.

As for the question of compressibility, let's take a brief look at one of the most exciting new fabrics to come on the market. It is known as Regulator insulation, a polyester-based fabric that is a closely related cousin of fleece. Regulator fabric is produced as a joint venture between Malden Mills and Patagonia. It offers warmth that is similar to fleece,

My Patagonia R2 middle layer, made with extremely light and compressible Regulator fabric.

but it is lighter, more compressible, more breathable, and faster drying.

The Regulator fabric is used in Patagonia's R2 Levitator pullover, which weighs all of 13 ounces yet offers the warmth of fleece that weighs at least 10 ounces more. Its ability to stuff down to the size of a large fist is also very appealing. It incorporates stretch panels along the sides, so it fits snugly around the torso and is incredibly comfortable. The Levitator is my middle layer of choice for three-season use. Patagonia offers Regulator in three different weights, simply called R1, R2, and R3, with R3 being the heaviest. All are extremely light for the warmth they offer, but R2 seems to make the best compromise between insulation and weight.

The makers of fleece have managed to derive a slew of different weights and styles from the same basic fabric, and have attached a dizzying array of names to them: power stretch, micro, heather, Patagonia's Activist and Synchilla, and so on. It's easy to become overwhelmed by the number of options. Simply choose the lightest fleece you can find that still has good insulative value. So far I've found nothing better than Regulator. However, if I'm going where I'm sure to encounter cold, numbing winds, I'll bring along a windproof fleece jacket instead. My favorite is the Mountain Hardwear Windstopper Tech jacket.

Any fleece top you get should weigh less than 15 ounces. You can keep the weight down by using pullover tops rather than jackets, reducing zipper weight. Fewer pockets and fewer technical features also save weight.

Outer Layer (Torso)

If you flip through almost any outdoor company's catalog, you'll find more options for outer-layer tops than anything else. The company wants you to have options for your outer shell based on the particular activity you will be pursuing, although there really are very few differences in the garments. Nearly all use some form of a waterproof-breathable fabric, which might lead you to believe that if you get anything else, Mother Nature might laugh you right out of the wilderness (if hecklers don't laugh you into it first). But as we'll see later in the chapter, there are other options.

Waterproof-Breathable Shells. The original Gore-Tex waterproof-breathable fabric has come a long way since its inception, and it gets better with every modification (although I remain a skeptic when it comes to waterproof-breathable fabrics, as I'll explain in just a bit). The latest incarnation is called Gore-Tex XCR (extended comfort range), which purports to be 25 percent more breathable than its predecessors.

I used to carry a typical waterproof-breathable shell that employed a three-layer Gore-Tex design. It took up a lot of room and weighed more than 2 pounds. (Of course, it would have weighed less without the eye-popping array of technical features that the manufacturer deemed important enough to include.) I kept the shell closed to keep the rain off, but after a while the inside of the shell began collecting condensed sweat, which eventually soaked through my interior layers and reached my skin. I quickly discovered that the shell didn't work as well as I had been led to believe. I expected to hike all day in the rain and stay dry. Not a chance.

Let's look at why waterproof-breathable fabrics are not necessarily the end-all of shell materials. To work properly, a waterproof-breathable fabric needs a difference in temperature (technically, vapor pressure) between one side and the other (see also Double-Wall vs. Single-Wall, in the chapter on Shelter). Water vapor can pass through a waterproof-breathable fabric to the outside as long as the inside is warmer than the outside. Usually, your skin heats up the inner side of the fabric enough for the vapor to pass through to the outside. But in hot climates, especially if they are humid as well, the garment can't breathe properly. Similarly, cold outside air can sometimes cool the inside of your jacket enough to inhibit the passage of vapor (unless your body is generating enough heat to create a large enough temperature differential). The result is condensation of that vapor on the inside of the fabric.

A waterproof-breathable fabric also needs a clear path for the water vapor from your body to escape. But rain droplets often stick to the outside of a shell. When this happens, the vapor's escape path is blocked. If enough of the shell is covered in rain droplets, you get the same result as with our first problem: interior condensation. Both of these problems worsen as the day goes on. You may start out the day with a dry skin and an eager spirit, but gradually the breathability of the shell degrades to where it becomes nearly useless in keeping you dry.

If you still want to go with a waterproof-breathable garment, one of your best options is to find a garment that uses Gore PacLite II, with its characteristic raised bumps on the inside. If I had to get a shell that was waterproof-breathable and had to accept the consequent weight and bulk, I would use PacLite. It works in the same way as regular Gore-Tex shells but doesn't use a liner. Most PacLite shells are simple in design, since manufacturers are finally recognizing that simpler is better (and lighter). Their average weight is around 1 pound: the Mountain Hardwear Aurora jacket (17 ounces); the North Face Ama Dablam jacket (15 ounces); the Lowe Alpine Adrenaline (a shade under 13 ounces).

An exceptional alternative to Gore-Tex in the waterproof-breathable department is the fabric used in the Frogg Toggs Pro Action rainsuit. The material is a polypropylene trilaminate that is waterproof and does a very good job with breathability—on par with Gore-Tex, if not better. The best part, however, is that the top and bottom together

A waterproof outer layer is essential on practically every trip. These are the extremely light Frogg Toggs.

weigh just under a pound. Even better, if you can believe it, is that the whole suit sells for only $72. The Frogg Toggs garments are rapidly gaining popularity with ultralight backpackers, and it's certainly a great option.

Another lightweight option is the Rain Shield Propore rainsuit. The material is waterproof and breathable, but is delicate and tears easily. The weight of the pants and jacket and individual stuff sacks together is an unbelievable 10 ounces.

Waterproof-Nonbreathable Shells. The best solution for the ultralight backpacker is actually the same solution as we found for tents: ventilation, and lots of it.

I find that pit zips, torso and extremity vents, and other zippered vents offer a much better way to go than relying on a breathable fabric. If you keep the vents open along with part of the front zipper and the wrist and waist cuffs, you'll be immeasurably drier and more comfortable than with any waterproof-breathable jacket all buttoned and zipped up. The vents are positioned so that rain doesn't get in when they are open. I've switched to a much lighter and more compressible waterproof—but nonbreathable—shell that incorporates many options for ventilation.

These waterproof shells are usually very simple in design, rarely weigh more than 10 ounces, and sometimes stuff right into one of their own pockets. They are made of a basic lightweight ripstop nylon and coated with waterproof polyurethane. I use the Mountain Hardwear Grade 5 anorak that is the size of a grapefruit when compressed and weighs 8 ounces after I've trimmed it of extraneous material.

The added advantage of any such waterproof shell is that it is also windproof. So for much less money and tens of ounces less than a fancy Gore-Tex jacket, my shell gives me all the protection I need.

Another option for reducing weight and bulk is to go for a shell that is breathable but not really waterproof. These nylon shells are usually coated with a durable water repellent (DWR) finish that does a pretty good job of keeping light, drizzle-like rain at bay. Eventually, moisture will begin to seep through the jacket, but you get an extremely breathable fabric in return. One of the best examples of this type of shell is Patagonia's

Essenshell pullover, which weighs 12 ounces. Another fine example is Marmot's Vindi windshirt, which weighs only 7 ounces.

I have to say that even after all the break-throughs and advances in waterproof-breathable designs, I'm sticking with my waterproof-nonbreathable shell. Granted, I'll be carrying around a little more sweat as the day wears on, but the overall savings in weight and bulk are just too good to pass up. And not a single tiny drop of rain is going to breach the fabric of my shell.

Almost all shells are treated on the outside with a DWR finish. This application keeps water from soaking into the outer layer of the shell, instead making it bead right off. Eventually the DWR finish will wear off, and the shell will become "wetted out." If the shell itself is completely waterproof, the water won't leak through to the inside, but it will make the shell heavier. Carefully monitor your shell for wet-out, and reapply a DWR finish, like Nikwax TX-Direct, when you notice it.

Pants

One of the first decisions backpackers have to make when packing their lower-body clothing is whether to bring shorts or pants, or both. Shorts are appealing because they represent athletic pursuits, and they are great for warm, sunny days. But in the interests of saving weight and bulk, you don't need them.

Pants offer a host of advantages over shorts that make them the clear winner. They provide shade for your legs, keeping them cooler and protecting them from sunburn. Pants give more protection against cuts and scratches, and against snakes and insects. Snakes always go for naked skin, and they

The Ex Officio Airstrip pants. *Courtesy Ex Officio*

On 95 percent of my trips, the only garments I bring for my legs are my Capilene long underwear and a very basic pair of breathable nylon pants. Practically every outdoor manufacturer offers a pair of nylon pants that work well. Look for pants that use a fairly thin, pliable nylon material without too many pockets and zippers. Stay away from convertible pants that become shorts, since the zipper that converts them adds unnecessary weight. Plus, they can chafe against the skin. An elasticized waist works better than a belt since it saves weight and is more comfortable beneath a pack's hip belt.

If I expect a lot of rain, I'll also bring some very light and simple rain pants. As with the top shell that I wear, these are polyurethane-coated nylon, making them nonbreathable but completely waterproof. Some rain pants have a full zipper up the sides, but these add weight and may allow water to leak through, so I do without. If it's at all possible, I leave my rain pants at home. I've hiked with wet legs on many occasions without any catastrophic results. Nylon dries extremely quickly, so if I hang up my pants overnight, they are almost always dry by morning.

Hat and Gloves

The main purposes of hats in the backcountry are to keep you warm, to keep you cool, and to stave off the rain. Let's talk about warmth first.

Because the brain needs vast quantities of blood to adequately oxygenate its tissues, the head is full of blood vessels. Many of these vessels lie close to the skin, so that when the outside temperature is below 98.6°F, the head gives off more heat than any other part

are known to smile quietly when they see someone coming along in shorts. I can't remember the last time I wore shorts while backpacking, and I've never felt the worse for it.

of the body. If you're cold, the best and easiest thing you can do to preserve warmth is to put on a hat that insulates well. I rarely go to sleep during a trip without a hat on, so that my body can be as efficient as possible in warming up the sleeping bag.

Fleece-lined hats are a perfect choice for trapping body heat before it can escape through the head. These are light, inexpensive, very warm, and comfortable. I like to use a hat that covers my eyes when I pull it down all the way so that the morning light won't interfere with my desire to sleep past dawn.

The other kind of hat you'll want to consider is one that protects you from both the sun and rain. Usually any hat that uses synthetic material and has broad flaps to cover your face, ears, and neck is sufficient. Find one that returns to its original shape after you wad it up in a ball. These come in a variety of styles, so try on a few and see what

feels comfortable and looks appealing. Baseball hats don't work very well because they don't cover the ears and neck.

I've always used a simple nylon hat with a 2-inch brim around the edge, because I like the shape and I can beat the heck out of it with no major consequences. It provides shade for my entire upper head regardless of the angle of the sun, and it gives me some protection against wetness. If it rains heavily, I opt for the hood of my rain jacket (with the fleece hat underneath if the temperature dips low). Many people like the Columbia sun hat, which is essentially a wide-brimmed baseball hat with a flap that runs over the ears and neck.

For your hands, all you need is a comfortable pair of fleece gloves. If your hands usually become cold quickly, get fleece gloves with a windproof membrane.

TRIMMING THE FAT

Now that you're totally outfitted for whatever nature can throw at you, it's time once again to engage in the meditative practice of trimming every possible ounce of weight.

Take all of your backpacking clothing and put it in a pile in front of you. All you need is a pair of scissors. A smaller pair works best because it can get into narrow places.

First, cut off all the labels. This includes those laundry and size tags and the ones that read "Made in Taiwan." It also includes manufacturer logo patches that are seemingly permanently stitched to the garment. This step does take patience because you don't want to cut the fabric of the garment itself. (If you are a surgeon, you'll have a

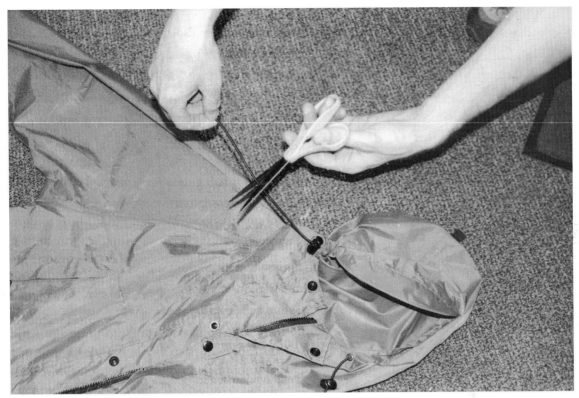

Scissors again make themselves useful in trimming off extraneous material from your clothing, like tags, tassles, and the unused ends of pull-cords.

much easier time of it.) Carefully cut a strand of stitching and slowly work your way around the label until it comes completely off. (Obviously, if the brand name is sewn right into the fabric, you're out of luck.)

The next step is to cut off the pull-strings from zippers and the extra length from drawstrings. On shells, you might find various mechanisms for tightening drawstrings around the hood, neck, and waist. The only thing you need to keep is a drawstring just long enough for you to grab hold of, and a plastic cord-lock to keep it from sliding back into the shell. If there is anything more than this, it can go. My Mountain Hardwear

Grade 5 jacket had an assembly for pulling on the drawstring without futzing with the cord-lock, and the end of the drawstring had a plastic cap. With nary a blink, I cut away the excess plastic and material, leaving just the basics. When I finished, the jacket was about 3 ounces lighter.

Cut off any unnecessary loops or hooks that are there to hang items from. Also cut off the piece of material that you'd use to hang the garment from a hook on the wall. Take a hard look at every feature. Anything that isn't part of the fiber of the garment should offer an enormous benefit, or off it comes. Try to get by without these features.

Added up, they can weigh a considerable amount.

Think about cutting away any extra pockets, leaving at least two on the pants and shell. Cut off extra pockets only if this will not damage the integrity of the garment itself. So if it means cutting a hole through the side of your shell, it's not worth it (although it would certainly help with ventilation!).

Finally, look for any other way that you can reduce weight. Use your own judgment on how much stuff you can trim before the garment reaches its ideal ultralight state. As you did with your tent, picture each piece of clothing the way Mr. Miyagi envisioned the bonsai tree in *The Karate Kid*. Somewhere within that jumble of loops, tags, patches, zippers, and drawstrings lies a potential member of the ultralight club, yearning to be free. It's your job to find the ultralight spirit in your jacket or your gloves or your pair of pants and set it free.

CHAPTER 6

THE REST OF THE GEAR

NOW THAT YOU'VE GATHERED TOGETHER a pack, sleeping bag, footwear, and clothing, it's time to turn our attention to everything else that you'll bring with you into the wilderness, from a stove to a bandanna to a first-aid kit. You can shave off several pounds when selecting the rest of the gear, and in this chapter we'll see how.

WHAT TO BRING

Here's a list of the additional gear you'll usually have in your ultralight pack:

- cook stove
- fuel container
- cook pot
- spoon
- lighter
- waterproof matches
- water treatment
- water containers
- towel
- bandanna
- first-aid kit
- soap
- sunscreen
- lip balm
- toothbrush
- toothpaste or tooth powder
- bug repellent
- stuff sacks
- compass
- maps
- sunglasses
- flashlight
- candle
- trekking poles
- multitool knife
- parachute cord
- duct tape

This is the most basic list of backpacking gear you would ever need; you really don't need any more than this. There are dozens of miscellaneous items you could add to this list, but practically all are luxuries or would be used only in specific or rare circumstances.

Let's now take each of the items on the list individually, and see how we can reduce their weight as much as is practical.

Cook Stove and Fuel Container

There are two primary types of backpacking stoves, based on the kind of fuel they use: liquid or gas. Both types offer distinct advantages and disadvantages.

I own both a liquid-fuel stove and a gas stove—the kind of trip I'm taking governs which one I bring. If it's a long trip to a remote area where I need to have extremely reliable equipment, I'll bring the liquid-fuel stove. For everything else, the gas-fuel stove comes with me because of its ease of use.

The MSR PocketRocket stove.

Liquid-Fuel Stoves. Stoves that use liquid fuel tend to be heavier than those that use gas, as does the fuel itself. But unlike the gas fuel (usually propane, butane, or a mixture), the liquid fuel is available just about everywhere. Many liquid stoves are multifuel. The MSR Whisperlite Internationale, perhaps the most popular backpacking stove in the world, can run on Coleman gas, white gas, kerosene, auto gasoline, and any other relatively clean-burning gas in the same octane range. This is especially useful if you are thru-hiking a long trail, where the gas fuels may be relatively scarce.

Another nice feature of liquid-fuel stoves is that, unlike the fuel canisters of gas stoves, you can reuse the fuel bottle. Liquid-fuel bottles usually come in three sizes (11, 22, and 33 fluid ounces). Experience will dictate exactly how much fuel your stove consumes. Bring only what you need, with a little extra built in for emergencies. MSR recommends 4 fluid ounces of fuel per person per day for their stoves.

An important feature of the Whisperlite Internationale is the shaker jet. The opening through which fuel emerges and is then ignited is extremely small, and is prone to collecting debris. The shaker jet is a weighted needle housed just inside the opening, and it can dislodge any debris if you simply shake the entire stove. This feature makes the stove

The MSR Whisperlite Internationale liquid-fuel stove.
Courtesy MSR Products (2)

extremely reliable; I've rarely heard of a Whisperlite clogging.

Gas-Fuel (Canister) Stoves. Gas-fuel stoves use either propane or butane, or a mix of both, carried in pressurized canisters that can be used only once and are then discarded. The lightest of these stoves, the Snow Peak Titanium GigaPower, weighs an unbelievable 2.5 ounces. Compare that to 14 ounces for the Whisperlite. A very light stove that's cheaper than the Titanium GigaPower (since

The MSR PocketRocket gas-fuel stove.

it uses stainless steel instead) is the MSR PocketRocket, weighing in at 3 ounces.

The advantage of the canister stoves is that they are very easy to use: just turn the valve, light the gas, and you're cooking—no pumping or priming required like with liquid fuel stoves.

With my gas-fuel stove, I almost always bring the smallest canister available. For the GigaPower or PocketRocket stoves, it's a 7.5-ounce canister (when full) that will last for 45 minutes at maximum output.

If you want to get just one stove for now, I recommend going with the Snow Peak GigaStove—the titanium version if you have the money, or the less expensive steel model, which weighs an ounce more. Either way,

when you combine this stove with a small gas canister, you will have one of the lightest and most compact stoves anywhere.

Other Stove Options. A favorite stove of many ultralight backpackers and the source of much debate is the Esbit stove. It's dirt cheap ($10), very compact, and weighs only about 3 ounces. The solid alcohol fuel tabs it uses weigh only half an ounce each, and the tabs burn up entirely, leaving no residue of any kind. The stove is very easy to set up and use, and almost nothing can go wrong with it.

Now for the flipside: the stove has only two settings, on and off. It takes about twice as long to boil water as with liquid-fuel or gas-fuel stoves, so you'll run through a lot of fuel tabs in even a short trip.

Another stove that burns alcohol (this time as a liquid) is the Mini-Trangia, also called the Trangia 28. The stove comes packaged with a pot, frying pan, pot lifter, and windshield, all nested in a compact bundle. The whole thing weighs 11.4 ounces. Again, you have to accept long boil times, but you still don't have to put up with any parts that could malfunction.

Cook Pot

I use my cook pot for boiling water, heating and eating food, drinking water and hot beverages, and bathing. This means I can leave all other cooking and eating paraphernalia at home. As for a lid, you have to assess the weight of the lid against the weight of the extra fuel you'll need to bring water to a boil, since boiling occurs more quickly when a lid is used. It's a close call, but the lid seems to lose this one; leave it at home.

I highly recommend spending the extra money for a titanium pot, which can be half the weight of a stainless steel pot. Cover the bottom of the pot with black stove paint to speed your boiling times. Black absorbs more heat, which in turn saves fuel. Try to buy a pot with a rounded bottom, which presents more surface area to the flame than a flat bottom and is easier to clean. MSR, Snow Peak, and Evernew make titanium pots that each weigh about 5 ounces.

Spoon

Lexan is the perfect material for eating utensils—light, durable, and cheap. My only

utensil is a single spoon, about the size of a teaspoon. I cut off about half of the handle, leaving just enough to grab without dipping my fingers into the food. Smooth off any sharp splinters from the edge.

If you want to consider yourself hard-core, don't bring any eating utensil at all. Use whatever you find along the trail or at the campsite as a utensil. Fallen twigs can be converted

For hard-core ultralight backpackers, use a twig instead of a spoon to stir and eat.

into chopsticks with just a little whittling. When you're done, you can burn the sticks if you're using a fire or return them to their natural environment. (The whittled ends could be perceived as trash, so if you want, break off these ends and pack them out.)

Lighter and Waterproof Matches

Carry a miniature lighter for lighting your stove. For a weight savings, bring one that is less than half full of fuel.

To save weight on the waterproof matches, you can cut the igniter strip from the box they come in and dump the strip, along with the matches, into a very small, zippered plastic bag. For a trip of less than a week, I bring about 15 matches for emergency use.

Water Treatment

I used to always carry a PUR Hiker water filter, because it is simple to operate and it provides clean, fresh-tasting water that I can drink right away. But I now use tiny, lightweight iodine tablets for water purification. Potable Aqua sells iodine tablets, along with ascorbic acid tablets that help cancel out the foul taste of the iodine.

The disadvantage is that you have to wait about half an hour after putting the iodine in the water before it is safe to drink (up to an hour if the water is very cold), but the relatively tiny weight and bulk are too attractive to pass up. My current ultralight pack is too small to justify hauling along a water filter, so I'm using the iodine tablets until someone invents a better system. However, for a very long-distance hike I would switch to a filter, because months of regularly ingesting iodine can pose a significant health risk.

Water Containers

The traditional water container has always been a rugged, cylindrical plastic bottle that is hard to pack and takes up just as much room empty as full. Water bladders are now giving the good old water bottle some stiff competition. Water bladders are pliable plastic bags, usually rectangular, with an opening at one end. You can attach a hose to the open end and snake it out of the pack and over your shoulder, where you can suck on it all day long. I love their shape, too. Water bladders fit nicely along the inside edge of the pack, and when empty and collapsed, take up hardly any space at all. And they weigh next to nothing.

Platypus makes a range of water bladders, called Hosers, that come in capacities of 1,

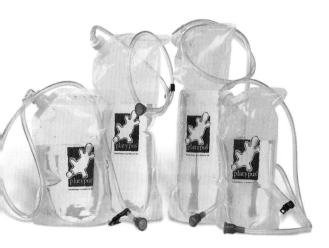

The Platypus Hosers. Courtesy Cascade Designs

1.8, 2, and 3 liters. I prefer the bladders made by Platypus because they retain odors the least, don't leak, and don't produce condensation on the outside of the bladder. On long trips with few water sources, I bring two 2-liter bladders. On shorter trips with plentiful water, I'll bring one 3-liter bladder. When full, that's enough water to last me an entire day, including cooking and cleaning. On exceptionally strenuous days, I have gone through a full 3-liter bladder by midafternoon, so it's not a bad idea to take along two bladders on every trip in case you need to carry more water.

Towel

You don't need much more than a bandanna to wipe yourself dry, but it's nice to have something a little more absorbent. I mostly use a small face towel, like the one you probably have in your bathroom. A great option is to get one of the super-absorbent towels sold in camping stores and cut out a 1-foot square to carry in your pack. When that piece gets old and smelly, simply cut out another one.

Bandanna

A bandanna can serve any number of purposes: straining leftover food, wrapping around an injury, protecting the neck from bugs and the sun, using as a prop for a magic trick. There is no special backpacking bandanna; the old-fashioned bandanna that you've seen in Westerns is just fine. I keep mine tied to a belt loop on my pants. Feel free to cut it into a smaller square to save a few fractions of an ounce.

First-Aid Kit

A first-aid kit is an absolute must in the wilderness. Although the human body is probably more reliable than any gear we might carry, it is still prone to breaking down every now and then.

If you are going solo or with only one other person, you need only a very basic kit. Mine includes the following:

- 2-inch-wide elastic bandage
- 1-inch micropore tape
- 2 safety pins
- 1 povidone-iodine pad
- 2 antibiotic ointments
- 2 antiseptic towelettes
- 10 adhesive bandages (various shapes and sizes)
- 4 strips of moleskin
- 1 gauze pad
- 1 nonadhesive pad
- 1 4- by 4-inch gauze sponge
- 6 two-tablet packages of assorted over-the-counter medicines, such as aspirin and indigestion tablets
- Multivitamin tablets

This is about as bare-bones a first-aid kit as you would want to use. Of course, if you're a member of a ten-person expedition to Baffin Island, you'll want something a little more substantial. As an instructor for backpacking outings, I carry a first-aid kit that includes just about every conceivable medical item to handle a wilderness emergency. It also weighs 2 pounds. My personal kit weighs about 5 ounces.

If you buy a commercially prepared first-aid kit, you'll find it usually comes with all sorts of straps, pockets, and elastic strips to hold things in place. When I bought one, I cut out about half of the original material, including two of the "pages" that held the items, the nylon webbing on the outside of the kit, and several pockets and elastic strips that I didn't need. All this trimming meant I had to condense the kit's contents into fewer pockets, but with a little shoving, I fit everything in. A good ready-made kit is the Optimist from Adventure Medical Kits. It weighs 6 ounces, and has a nice selection of items for most minor incidents encountered in the backcountry.

Toiletries

This includes soap, sunscreen, lip balm, toothbrush, toothpaste or tooth powder, and bug repellent. No matter what kind of container the liquids come in, I always transfer them to small, plastic bottles with a screwdown lid. I bring only enough to last me for the trip. If you're going out for three days, pack enough soap for three days and no more.

As you gain experience, you'll learn to gauge more precisely how much of each item you'll need. If it turns out that there are more mosquitoes than you had anticipated on your trip in the northern Sierras in August, you'll know for next time to bring along a little more.

For soap, I always use the liquid kind. Ask backpackers which soap they use, and the vast majority will reply with the name long associated with backcountry hygiene: Dr. Bronner's. This amazing stuff can be used to brush your teeth, clean your pots and pans, shave, and relieve insect bites, along with a slew of other uses. I'm not certain what all the writing is about on the bottle, but the stuff works, and works well.

Stuff Sacks

Many ultralight backpackers don't use stuff sacks at all, which saves weight and ensures that there is no dead air space in their packs. Others like to compartmentalize all of their gear into stuff sacks so they can find it easily and so it doesn't shift inside the pack. (See about stuff sacks, page 16.)

My sleeping bag is compressible enough that I can get it to fit tightly into the bottom of the pack with no stuff sack. And rather than putting my clothing in a stuff sack, I prefer to use the clothing to fill in spaces around the edges of the pack. But if I want to pack several clothes items together, I use an Eagle Creek Pack-It Compressor (described below).

I use a stuff sack for my food because I want to keep it all in the same place and have easy control over how the weight of the food is distributed. Plus, I don't want to go digging for my granola bar all the way in the bottom of the pack when I get hungry.

Eagle Creek's Pack-It Compressor is a terrific invention that I highly recommend to ultralight backpackers. It is essentially a large, reinforced plastic, waterproof zippered bag, but with a key additional feature: it has a one-way air valve at the bottom of the bag, so that when you roll it from the top, all the air inside is squeezed out—leaving, in effect, a vacuum-packed stuff sack. I've found nothing else that can compress gear into such a tight space. Clothing can be compressed to where it doesn't take up much more than half the space it would use in a regular stuff sack.

I've now started using a Pack-It Compressor for my food instead of a standard stuff

The Eagle Creek Pack-It Compressor.
Courtesy Eagle Creek, Inc.

sack, and you can also use it for some of the more compressible sleeping bags. The compressors come in only two sizes, both quite large. If the company ever comes out with compressors in a variety of sizes, you could conceivably pack all your gear in these and carry them in a backpack made of mesh that would weigh just a few ounces.

Another ultralight option is the GoLite Stow Sack. The sacks come in a variety of sizes, all of which employ a very thin and light ripstop nylon. The sacks range in weight from half an ounce to an ounce.

Compass

At the risk of offending some traditional backpackers, you don't need to bring a compass on every single trip. If you'll be staying on trails in a well-traveled area that you are familiar with and is not too remote, you simply don't need a compass. You might enjoy having one to help determine the name of the peak you see off in the distance, but if you use your common sense and don't plan to

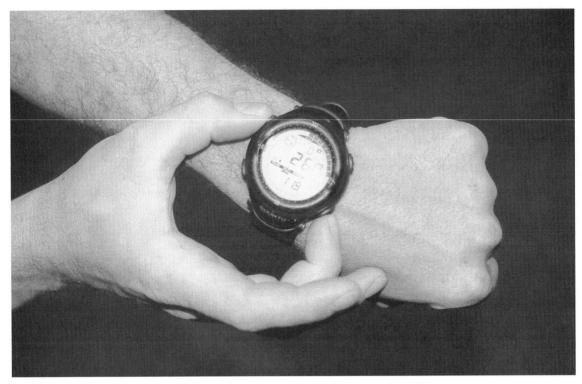

The Suunto Vector all-in-one watch.

leave the trail, the compass is not an essential item.

With that said, I bring a compass along on every trip—but only because it's a part of my watch. I wear a Casio Pathfinder, which includes a compass, barometer, temperature gauge, and altimeter. Suunto also makes watches with compasses.

However, if you're heading into territory that's unfamiliar to you or where you might not be hiking on an established trail, definitely bring a compass. Please use your best judgment on this issue. Bring a compass if you feel there's the smallest chance you may need it. Use a compass that is as compact as possible while still giving accurate readings. I bring a Suunto orienteering-style compass if I'm heading off to a remote location I've not visited before.

Maps

Some people get a little map-crazy and bring along topo maps, trail maps, small-scale and large-scale maps, road maps, and maps from space. I usually carry enough 15-minute U.S. Geological Survey (USGS) maps to cover the area of my hike. Each of these maps represents an area that measures 15 minutes of longitude by 15 minutes of latitude. The 7.5-minute USGS maps don't cover enough area, and are more detailed than I need.

Maps made by Tom Harrison (see appendix list of manufacturers and suppliers) are nice because they are waterproof and tear-proof and because they cover areas by regional interest, meaning your hike will almost always be entirely on a single map. As with the compass, if I am familiar with an area and I'm not going off-trail, I won't bring a map at all.

Sunglasses

High-quality sunglasses are important to me. I don't want the lenses to get scratched, and I want a comfortable fit that will stay that way over a hot, sweaty, 20-mile day. Get sunglasses with lightweight plastic frames. If you can afford it, polarized lenses provide unparalleled clarity that just seems to make everything look better. I used to wear a neck cord to secure the glasses, but when I tried going without the cord, it didn't seem to matter, so I don't bother with one anymore.

Flashlight

The ideal ultralight flashlight is a compact penlight, like the Mini Maglite. It uses a single AAA battery and provides adequate light for most purposes. If possible, use a lithium battery instead of an alkaline battery because the lithium weighs half as much and lasts twice as long.

You could also use an LED flashlight, like the Photon Micro-Light that weighs all of 1/4 ounce, or the brighter but heavier CMG Infinity Task Light (1 ounce without its single AA battery). Neither of these gives off as much light as a regular bulb, but the LED lasts far longer and uses less battery power. They both come in a variety of colors of light, but I recommend white because it displays colors as your eyes see them in daylight.

Most headlamps are too heavy and bulky for ultralight backpacking. But if you really like their functionality, try the Petzl Micro, which weighs just 3.2 ounces or the Petzl Tikka, just 2.5 ounces.

Candle

I like to have a candle handy in case my flashlight stops working. I also light it when I cook and eat dinner to save flashlight battery power. You could certainly go without a candle, but I feel more comfortable in the wilderness when I know I have an alternative source of light.

Birthday candles are great because they are light, cheap, and small. And when it's cold and wet and you miss home, you can pretend it's your birthday. To get the most light out of a candle, place your stove's windscreen around it as a reflector.

Trekking Poles

Trekking poles offer some wonderful benefits, not the least of which is how much weight they can take off of the lower part of your body. The poles also provide extra points of balance, very helpful in fording streams. These virtues, and others, are discussed in detail in chapter 9, Walking.

Multitool Knife

The Swiss Army knife has always been a favorite among backpackers for its compactness and versatility. Multitool knives from Leatherman and other manufacturers have now replaced the traditional Swiss Army knife as the best choice. The obvious reason is that these newer knives have a great pair of pliers that fits snugly into the tool when closed. Leatherman and Buck both make smaller versions of their heftier multitools, which have everything you might need on a backpacking trip.

Get a tool that has a big enough blade to be of practical use. If it is too small, you won't be able to cut things like wood or nylon webbing or fish heads. Ounce for ounce, these smaller multitools offer a lot more versatility than the Swiss Army knives.

Cord

Here's yet another multiuse item. You can use utility cord to lash items to your pack, to guy out your tent, and to set up a clothesline, among many other uses. I bring 25 feet of it on my trips. Wrap it as tightly as you can so it takes up little room and won't become loose and drape the rest of your pack's contents in a tangled nightmare.

Duct Tape

Duct tape may very well be the most useful and practical item in your pack—but one you will probably use only rarely. It can make your life immeasurably easier if something goes wrong with a particular piece of gear. However, there's obviously no sense in bringing an entire roll.

Most people in the know carry a length of duct tape wrapped around their trekking poles. Just unwrap pieces of it if you need it for a repair. I wrap a 2-inch-wide segment around one pole, and then tear the tape down the middle to make two 1-inch-wide pieces. I then wrap one of them around the other pole.

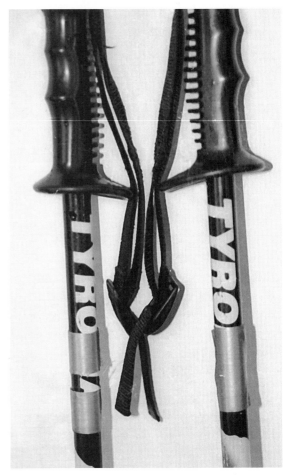

Wrap different widths of duct tape around your trekking poles.

TRIMMING THE FAT

Even after you've selected the lightest gear you can find that does the job, it's still possible to shave the weight down a bit more. Following are a few ideas, and you'll come up with more on your own.

Take any stuff sack you plan to use and cut off all labels and tags. If there is a handle attached to the bottom, away it goes.

Also cut off the extra drawstring material (and burn the ends to prevent fraying), leaving just enough to open the sack fully.

I always try to get a single broad map that covers my entire hike and then cut off all sections of the map that I won't need (including margins). You can even photocopy the relevant map section and scale it down by 10 or 20 percent or more to further lessen the weight and bulk.

As for your toothbrush, you can use the old trick of sawing it in half. And use tooth powder instead of paste, since it's lighter and can be stored in a lightweight plastic bag.

After I cut half of the handle off the lightweight plastic spoon I carry, I take the time to drill a few holes along the portion of the handle that remains. This might seem extreme, but it's actually an important step to take if you want to completely assume the commitment to being an ultralight backpacker.

Yes, the weight savings are negligible, but I don't drill those holes to save weight. I do it because ultralight backpacking is a state of mind. It means not letting a single extra fraction of an ounce get away with hitching a ride on my back. I want to get things to their absolute cleanest, lightest, and purest, and if that means drilling small holes into the already shortened handle of a spoon, then that's exactly what I'll do.

WHAT TO LEAVE AT HOME

You'll see backpackers carrying any number of items they could really do without. Here are a few common ones.

Groundsheet

The purpose of a groundsheet is to keep whatever you put on it clean and dry. If you're using a tarp for your shelter, you'll need a groundsheet to keep your sleeping bag and other gear dry if it rains. Use one made of lightweight polyethylene. This material can rip easily, but anything more durable becomes too bulky and heavy.

I've never used a groundsheet with a tent, and haven't suffered for it. The bottom of the tent may be wet and dirty in the morning, but a few good shakes usually cleans it up adequately. Don't be fooled into thinking that since a groundsheet adds only a few ounces, you might as well bring one along. Part of being an ultralight backpacker is breaking away from that kind of false justification.

Weight savings: 3 to 6 ounces.

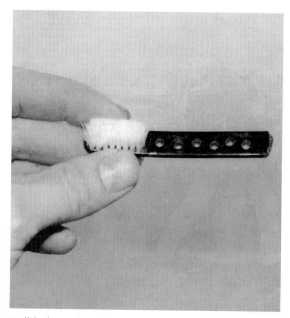

Drill holes in handles when light weight, not strength, is important.

Stuff extra clothing into the base of your pack and use it as a pillow.

Pillow

A backpacking pillow is strictly a luxury item, on par with backpacking espresso machines and electric foot warmers. Making your own pillow in the wilderness is easy: just take all the clothes you aren't wearing to bed, shove them in a stuff sack, and put it under the hood of your sleeping bag. Voilà, instant pillow. If you want something cozier, wrap a fleece garment around the stuff sack. If you don't have a stuff sack, shove the clothing directly into the sleeping-bag hood. If your bag doesn't have a hood, put the clothes in the bottom of your pack and use the pack as a pillow.

Weight savings: 3 ounces.

Camp Chair

Some backpackers justify the added bulk and weight of a fold-up camp chair by saying that after a hard day of hiking, they want to be comfortable. Well, that day of hiking wouldn't be so hard if they had left the camp chair at home. I've never had much of a problem sitting on a rock or against a tree or on the ground, and there's no way my ultralight backpack could accommodate something like this anyway. That's the beauty of using a small pack: it forces you to find out what your priorities are. Should I take the sleeping pad or the camp chair? That's a fairly easy decision, and your body will thus hike unburdened by an unnecessary luxury item.

Weight savings: 8 to 15 ounces.

Books, Games, Entertainment

Since backpacking can entail a good bit of down time, it's easy to find yourself getting restless. I remember a time when I dreaded getting to camp in the middle of the after-

THE ULTRALIGHT WAY: Back to Nature

We finally arrive at perhaps the most sensitive subject of all. The more discerning of you might have noticed the absence of toilet paper from our list of gear at the beginning of this chapter. A typographical error, perhaps? Alas, no.

I remember my greatest fear before leaving on the Outward Bound trip that introduced me to backpacking was what to do with number two. Toilet paper was not on their list either. Please don't tell anyone this, but I managed to last eight full days without going. It's a documented sociological fact that when you get people away from the wonders of plumbing and toilet paper, many of them tend to freak out.

As it turns out, evacuating your digestive system without the aid of conventional services really isn't all that bad. Find a nice spot away from water and trails, dig a hole with a branch or your trekking pole, do your business, clean yourself up, and go on your merry way. To accomplish that second-to-last chore, you can use leaves, twigs, or some water cupped in your hand. I bring along some liquid soap that I use with a little water, and then pat dry with some leaves, or with my bandanna if there's nothing else. Of course, I won't then go and blow my nose with it until I've had the chance to clean it with soap and water. Don't forget to cover up the hole before you leave.

If you absolutely cannot do without toilet paper, at least don't take an entire roll. Take just a few sheets and keep it in the zippered plastic bag with your toiletries. You'll also have to bring along another plastic bag for packing out the soiled toilet paper, since we never want to leave any of it behind.

noon, wondering how I would entertain myself until it was time to go to sleep. After all, setting up camp, cooking, and eating take only an hour or two, and you can enjoy the views for only so long before your brain needs some other stimulation. Thus many backpackers bring something to read. Nowadays, when I see a backpacker reading a book, the only thing I see written on it over and over is the word *heavy*.

However, the primary reason why I don't bring a book or other form of entertainment isn't the weight. I've come to realize that our brain's constant need for stimulation is the product of living in a world of television shows and billboards and shopping malls, where

being bored is akin to being locked in a dungeon. Most of us hardly ever give ourselves time to just enjoy a little peace and quiet.

The downtime on a backpacking trip is the perfect opportunity to find and accept the peace that many of us lack in our day-to-day lives. Reading a book can be just another distraction from the serenity that surrounds us in nature. Believe me, it's hard work to not give in to your brain's need for stimulation for several hours. But it can be immensely rewarding once you push beyond that need. Some of my most potent memories of the outdoors are of just sitting on a rock and opening up my senses to the world around me.

Weight savings: 10 ounces.

CHAPTER 7
FOOD

A S I PERUSE THE AISLES OF MY LOCAL GRO-
cery store, I keep a watchful eye out for
food items I can bring on my next backpacking
trip. I factor in several criteria before I choose
anything that goes into my ultralight food bag.
In addition to nutritional value and ease of
preparation, I'm always considering bulk,
taste, price, practicality, and of course, weight.

Thinking about these factors actually
makes shopping easy, because there aren't
that many choices that strike an acceptable
balance between them all. Sure, ice cream
tastes good, especially if it contains as many
different forms of chocolate as possible, but
is obviously impractical for a backpacking
trip. Likewise, a Cornish game hen would
provide plenty of protein, but my little camping stove and pot just isn't going to handle
it—not to mention the bulk and weight.

BUILDING BLOCKS OF ULTRALIGHT FOOD

When we walk into a grocery store, we want
to use our "food radar" to hone in on items
that satisfy all of our criteria. To start working on building that radar, let's study each
of the factors that go into deciding appropriate ultralight backpacking foods. Then
we'll look at specific foods that work well for
ultralight travel.

Nutritional Value

Examining every aspect of a particular food's
nutritional content is better left to the skills
of a trained nutritionist. Before I embarked
on an extended hike along the Pacific Crest
Trail, I spent a lot of time studying nutrition, and I began seeing those little nutrition
labels on food packaging in my dreams. I
realized later that I could have spent my time
on more useful preparations, because you
really don't need to know that much to pick
the right backpacking foods.

Of course, if you're the analytical type, then by all means spend as much time as you want studying what foods to bring. Some people love the idea of graphs and charts and every other conceivable means of examining a food's nutritional content before choosing it for their expedition, while others (including myself) stop by a village grocery store on the way to the trailhead and pick up whatever seems to fit the bill.

The constituents of food can essentially be organized into three broad categories: fat, protein, and carbohydrates.

Fat is something like money stored in a jar and buried in the backyard. Your body stores it in case unexpected circumstances arise and it desperately needs to fuel its ongoing activity.

Protein is like a regular savings account. Muscle and body tissue are provided by your body converting protein, but it's not the primary source of energy. Sometimes, if there's too much protein, your body can afford to store the protein as fat (like adding to the buried jar).

Carbohydrates are your checking account —the stuff you use every day in producing the energy you need for daily activities.

As backpackers, we are mostly concerned with the carbohydrate value of food. When we're pounding up a rugged trail, it's the carbos we've ingested that are going to get us up that hill. If you make only one nutritional consideration when selecting your backpacking food, it should be looking for foods that are high in carbohydrates. If you want to take it a step further, look for foods high in complex carbohydrates that give you more energy for a longer period of time. We'll talk about specific high-carbo foods a little later.

For breakfast and throughout the day, eating foods high in complex carbos is my main objective. For dinner, I concentrate a little more on protein, so that my body has the tools it needs to rebuild my muscles overnight. As for fat, you really only need to concern yourself with it if you're going on an extended winter trip or a thru-hike on a long-distance trail. A long-distance thru-hiker will probably lose at least 15 pounds from the beginning of the trail to the end, so fat becomes more of a consideration. During the last month before I started on a long-distance hike, I ate nothing but fat, fat, and more fat to have enough long-term storage for my body to tap into.

You also want to consider the caloric content of food. Calories are like the dollar bills in your various accounts, the units that actually provide you with energy. The more strenuous the activity, the more calories your body needs. While hiking, an ultralight backpacker will burn about 250 calories an hour.

All in all, you should create a backpacking diet that will provide you with about 3,000 to 4,000 calories per day, two-thirds of which should be in the form of carbohydrates. I've found that this comes out to roughly 1 to 1½ pounds of food per day if the day's hike is about 5 miles or less. On trips where I hike close to 20 miles a day, that figure rises to 2½ pounds.

Weigh your food bag to roughly measure if you're in the ballpark with your weight per day. If it comes out to less than a pound a day, go back and recheck your meals. It you end up with 5 pounds per day, I hope you're also bringing enough shelter for the army you're obviously feeding.

Ease of Preparation

Before my ultralight days, I took a trip into the mountains of western Colorado with a backpacking couple that I knew from work. As I drove to the trailhead, my pack sat next to me like a giant red blob. After meeting up with the couple at the trailhead, I saw that their packs made mine look like a dainty little purse.

We started down the trail and after only 2 or 3 miles, Ken announced that we had arrived at our campsite. I sat on a rock and watched in amazement as he and his wife constructed a kitchen so elaborate that I imagined they were preparing to serve a gathering of heads of state. Stoves, ovens, coffee makers, spices and sauces, assorted knives and other cutlery, a bottle of wine . . . the stuff just kept coming. They spent the rest of the day preparing what was surely the most lavish and extravagant spread the Rockies had ever seen. Ease of preparation? I don't think so.

I have reached a happy state at the opposite end of the spectrum. I eat because I need the nourishment, and that's about it. That's not to say that I take only a bag of unrefined wheat and whatever scraps I can find in the cupboard; it's just that my main priority isn't indulging my palate. Basically, my meal preparation at its most complicated involves ripping open a paper packet, dumping its contents into a pot, mixing, and heating.

As for cold foods, I just open the plastic bag, pull out a chunk, morsel, or scoop of whatever it contains, and shovel it in. The food tastes fine, and it keeps things simple and lightweight. I look for good foods that I can eat without preparation. Baby carrots come to mind right away. Just dump as many as you want into a zippered plastic bag for your hike. Beef jerky, dried fruit, and gorp are other no-prep foods.

Low Bulk

You have to take into account how much space your food will require. Let's use Rice Krispies treats as an example. They're certainly light, taste good, contain several important nutritional elements, and are cheap and easy to prepare. But they take up a heck of a lot of room for what you get. I once had a backpacking student who brought a stack of Rice Krispies treats that filled more than half of her food bag. The separation was a sad one as the student bid farewell to the treats, but she definitely ate a lot better as a result.

Your food bag has only limited space, and you need to use every cubic inch of it as wisely as possible. Think about averaging out the nutritional content of your food over those cubic inches and raising the average as high as possible by reducing your food's bulk.

One easy way to achieve this is to strip everything you get of all its packaging. Beef jerky, for example, sometimes comes in stiff plastic packaging that takes up much more space than the jerky by itself. So I transfer the jerky to a lighter and less bulky zippered plastic bag. Always get rid of the commercial packaging, and use the plastic bags as if they grew on trees. If you need the instructions on the box, cut them out and put them in the bag too.

You can also reduce bulk by breaking up the units that the food comes in. For example, I tear up the beef jerky into little pieces so that it takes up even less room. Peanuts, raisins, and such are great because there's very little dead air space among all the pieces. Big Bavarian pretzels out of the bag are too bulky, but you can easily break them into little pieces before packing so they take up less space.

Creative packing is another important element in reducing bulk. If your cook pot has any extra space, fill it with food in zippered plastic bags. These bags come in different thicknesses; use the thinnest, lightest ones that won't pose a risk of breaking.

Good Taste

I'm willing to accept a little blandness for the sake of fully satisfying the other criteria for ultralight food. At the same time, I believe that every backpacker should be able to pick one food item to bring along simply because it tastes good. I've seen people bring along everything from smoked oysters to chocolate-covered raisins to Jolly Rogers candy. Just don't go overboard with it.

Many people like to bring taste-enhancing items like spices, soy sauce, or olive oil. If you want to bring spices, transfer them into zippered plastic bags. Sauces and oils should be carried in one of those small Nalgene containers (about the size of a film canister) with the secure screw-down lid. Bring only as much spice or flavoring as you'll need.

As for the rest of the food, there's no reason to bring anything you have to gag down. I'll never forget the awful experience of taking a break during the second day of a trip and pulling out one of those highly touted energy bars. It was the most vile thing I had ever tasted. After gagging down a third of it, I swore off energy bars for good—and I've kept my vow. There's no need to succumb to the promises of magical foods if you can't stomach them. Every item in your food bag should be one that you can comfortably eat.

There's now a horde of energy bars on the market with promises of complete nutrition. But you can get vitamins and minerals from a vitamin pill that takes up a fraction of the space of an energy bar. The high protein content of some bars can be a benefit, but I'd much rather get it from sources like raisins, nuts, and beef jerky. If you've found an energy bar that you are partial to, then go for it. But if you're wondering whether or not to jump on the energy bar band-wagon, my opinion is to look for energy in more promising and palatable places.

Be sure to sample any food before you put it in your pack. Also, the same food will taste different depending on the manufacturer, so take the time to find a brand you like. For example, some brands of dried fruit taste better than others.

It's a good idea to vary your food selection from trip to trip—don't always bring carrots, raisins, and beef jerky. On almost every trip, I experiment with a new kind of food, just to see if I like it enough to make it a staple. My latest great find is the tasty sugar snap pea. Satisfying your taste buds is a constant process. I have core food items that I bring every time, but a quarter to a third of the food I bring changes on every trip.

Reasonable Price

I am a budget-conscious shopper. You won't see me out on the trail with truffles, foie gras, or caviar (although I did bring smoked salmon on one trip). The nice thing about backpacking food is that it lasts forever, so you can buy a lot of it in bulk. About every six months, I'll go to my local grocery warehouse of massive excess and buy such things as 2-pound tubs of trail mix, boxes of noodle soup packets, and gallon containers of jerky. These foods could last through a nuclear war.

Usually, good backpacking food is some of the cheapest stuff on the grocery shelves. If I'm prudent, I can spend less than $5 for a day's worth of backpacking food. For long-distance trails, I've averaged just a shade over $5 a day. Just remember these three words—buy in bulk.

THE ULTRALIGHT WAY: A BACKPACKER'S CONFESSION

I have a little secret. I always carry one item in my pack that might not be loaded with nutrition and that may be taking up space that could be used more efficiently—but that nicely caters to my junk food cravings.

For me, it's always been either those rolled-up fruit leathers or chocolate chip cookies. I've found that spoiling myself with one food item of luxury does wonders for my morale. For those times when it's been raining all day and I've walked 15 miles uphill to reach camp, there's nothing better than a perfectly timed chocolate chip cookie break.

It is at this point that I would like to express my sincere dislike of those racks and racks of freeze-dried food packets you'll find at any outdoors store. These products thrive on the fact they are easy to cook—but at what price? Not only are they ridiculously expensive—6 or 7 dollars for something that would cost about 18 cents in the grocery store—but the contents usually taste like hot cardboard. The names on the labels sound enticing, but save your money. There's plenty of much more satisfying food on the shelves of your local grocery store. (We'll look at some examples near the end of this chapter.)

Practicality

This subject ties in with all the other criteria, and is quite subjective. For an ultralight backpacker, practical food means all of the things we've already talked about, but mostly it means that the process of providing yourself with nourishment is as painless and straightforward as possible. Roasted peanuts? Practical. Fresh-roasted garlic cloves? Not practical. One quick rule you can employ is that anything that can get mushed is not practical. Raisins? Practical. Grapes? Not practical. Get the idea?

Practical food also covers stuff that will keep, even during long and sweaty days where the temperature inside your pack goes into triple digits. If you bring along anything fresh, you better eat it quickly or you'll be spawning a rainbow of fungus in your food bag. Before including food in your bag, try to imagine its life span between the time you pack it and the time you eat it. Imagine what fresh Stilton cheese will go through on a four-day hike through Death Valley. This might appear to be an obvious point, but I've seen some nasty concoctions out there because people weren't thinking beyond refrigerators and air-conditioning.

Low Weight

At last we come to the crucial factor in determining ultralight food. The idea is to pack in as much nutrition, taste, and value as you can into the lightest possible unit of food. The problem is that foods with high nutritional content are usually also heavy. Vitamin pills are a notable exception.

I usually don't take vitamin pills on a daily basis, trying instead to get what my body needs from the food I eat. But vitamins are very useful to the ultralight backpacker. In just a tiny pill that weighs less than an ounce, you get an entire day's worth of essential nutrition. I take one multivitamin pill per day on my backpacking trips. That way, there isn't so much pressure to obtain all the vitamins and minerals that I need strictly from the food I eat.

Removing the packaging from any food you buy cuts down not only on its bulk, but also on its weight. There's nothing much lighter than a zippered plastic bag, like a Ziploc, for packaging and carrying food. Use these bags for everything, including instant noodle and rice meals. Some meals, like macaroni and cheese, come in two separate packages—the macaroni in the box itself, the cheese in a separate pouch. Tear open the pouch and dump the cheese right along with the macaroni into a plastic bag.

Keep your ultralight radar on and try to find ways to reduce packaging as much as possible. Sometimes you can put different food items together in the same plastic bag. There's really no need to separate raisins and peanuts, since they go together as perfectly as . . . well, raisins and peanuts. You can combine beef jerky with just about anything, since you can easily pull out the pieces of jerky without disturbing the rest of the bag's contents.

A simple but not too obvious way of saving weight on food is to gorge yourself when you have the opportunity. Now, this doesn't mean you should stuff down a couple bags of pork rinds and a basket of French fries; but a healthy, nutritionally beneficial meal before setting out on the trail can do wonders for your energy level as well as allowing you to cut down on that day's food supply.

I discovered this technique of "camelling up" on food along the Pacific Crest Trail, taking full (and almost stomach-exploding) advantage of any restaurant within a few miles of the trail. Anytime you have the chance to have a full, healthy meal without adding any weight to your pack, take it and thank the gods for the opportunity.

Try to judge when you'll be exiting from the backcountry so that you can have another stomach-filling meal right after the trip. If I plan on getting back to the trailhead at around 11 o'clock in the morning, then I only need to pack that morning's breakfast and don't need to carry a lunch.

Use the same technique for water, chugging as much as you can at water sources. That way, you don't have to take quite as much water with you when you leave the source.

AND NOW . . . THE FOOD

Following are some food options that have proven themselves in meeting the criteria for a good ultralight food—high nutritional content, easy preparation, compact, tasty, cheap, practical, and light. It includes foods that have always served me well and ones that have worked for many fellow ultralight

Camelling up on food and water before hitting the trail means not having to carry as much of either in your pack.

backpackers. Feel free to create your own menus, and experiment as much as you like.

Rice and Pasta

The various forms of rice and pasta are among the most popular backpacking foods available—easy to cook, with countless different ways of preparation. They are high in complex carbohydrates, providing you with the energy stores you'll need the following day.

On the backpacking trips that I instruct, we almost always make our version of pasta primavera on one night during the two- or three-day outing. We bring along plenty of fresh vegetables, like red and green peppers, onions, zucchini, and squash. We'll also throw in some fresh garlic, olive oil, and a couple cans of chicken. The resulting dish is close to divine—but ultralight it's not. I'd never haul all that stuff on a private trip.

Instead, I have sworn allegiance to Lipton's instant rice and pasta meals. They come in a variety of flavors, are incredibly easy to prepare, and taste pretty darn good. There's not much more involved than dumping the contents into a boiling pot of water, stirring, and eating.

Another favorite in the pasta family is the venerable macaroni and cheese. The one notable drawback is that it leaves a nasty residue on the inside of the pot, which means that all the dishes you prepare after that one will taste a little cheesy. Kraft Cheesy Pasta is probably the most popular brand.

Favored among backpackers and college freshmen alike is the ever-expanding selection of ramen noodles. Because they're hard and usually rectangular, they can be difficult to pack, so I always break them up into pieces for space efficiency. I find that they are not as satisfying as the Lipton dinners, but they always taste good and can provide some variety.

Granola

I used to always prepare granola cereal for breakfast, using powdered milk and mixing it all in my cook pot. But even the simple process of mixing in the powdered milk, eating the granola, and cleaning up began taking away from my all-important early-morning hiking time. Now, I just eat a couple of granola bars for breakfast and hit the trail within half an hour of waking up.

Most of the granola sold in grocery stores has been severely processed, so I like to get mine from an organic or whole foods market (although I've brought along the Nature Valley granola bars sold in grocery stores and have been very happy with them). You can buy granola either in solid bars or loose in cereal form. The loose kind is easier to pack but a little trickier to eat.

Dried Fruit

My favorite dried fruit has always been raisins. With any dried fruit, one option is to cut it into little pieces and mix them with nuts, M&Ms, or any other ingredient that you think go well together. Gorp (Good Old Raisins and Peanuts) has always been a backpacker's staple, but it's only a starting point for combining food items into a trail mix. You can also throw in coconut flakes, sunflower seeds, chocolate chips, granola, or about anything else you've developed a taste for.

I almost always bring along a couple pieces of fruit leather. Instead of the highly processed kind from the grocery store, I get mine from a whole foods market. If you have a dehydrator, you can make your own by pureeing the fruit in a blender and spreading the resultant paste in the machine.

Meat

The process of drying strips of beef into jerky was one of the most notable inventions of early pioneers. I don't think I've ever gone on a trip without some jerky in my food bag. For variety, I bring slices of hard salami, which seems to last longer than other cured meats. I know this from the experience of pondering the opalescent qualities of the mold that spread over my smoked turkey during one particularly unfortunate trip.

For your first or second night's meal, you can also bring along some canned chicken (transferred to a zippered plastic bag, of course). Dump it into your pot and cook it along with whatever else is already in there. Beyond the second night, I wouldn't trust the freshness of the uncanned chicken.

Vegetables

Fresh vegetables aren't the most practical food to bring along unless you consume them quickly. Anything fresh is sure to have a relatively high water content, so the dry version is always more ultralight-friendly. There's nothing wrong with bringing along a couple of fresh vegetables as long as they don't take up space that might be occupied by something you need later on.

You can also prepare a small salad at home, place it in a zippered plastic bag, pour in a little dressing, and compress the bag as tightly as you can. A regular bowl of salad can be compressed into a tight wad that takes up very little space and can be allowed to expand once you're ready to eat it.

Instant potatoes are a particular favorite of many ultralight backpackers. They come in a flaky or powdered form that you mix into heated water.

Cheese

Cheese is one of the few dairy products that won't make you regret you have the sense of smell after a few days out in the baking heat of summer. Of course, that rule applies only to certain types of cheese; a nice chunk of Roquefort might be great after a French meal, but not after three days of sitting in your hot, dank pack. I usually bring the simplest form of cheese I can find, the venerable Kraft American slice, which is processed and thus virtually immune to outdoor temperatures.

Unrefrigerated cheddar, Monterey Jack, and Swiss will generally last for several days before succumbing to the ravages of mold.

Drink Mixes

I like water. A clear mountain stream is the source for some of the cleanest, best-tasting water on earth. So why mask that pureness with Gatorade or Kool-Aid mix? Well, if you're using iodine to treat your water, a flavored drink mix is going to taste infinitely better than the treated water. Also, many drink mixes provide a host of minerals and nutrients that can help your body. Emer'gen-C, made by Alacer, is a drink mix that packs a healthy punch. It contains 28 different electrolytes as well as a host of essential nutrients, and comes in a variety of flavors. MET-Rx, Gatorade, and several other brands offer good flavored drink mixes.

CHAPTER 8
HEALTH AND SAFETY

NATURE, WHEN LEFT TO ITS OWN devices, can be awfully unfriendly if you have no idea what you're doing. Luckily, our best tools for keeping the unpredictable dangers of nature at bay are our own deepest instincts. The survival instinct of the human mind may be the most powerful force around, greater than any bear or flood or tornado. And spending time in the wilderness makes us rely on it much more than when we're in civilization.

My first few trips into the wilderness were pretty fearful events. I had little idea of what I might encounter, and without all the protections I had grown up with, I felt vulnerable and naked. With every new experience came a barrage of "what-if" scenarios, and I had no shortage of them on those initial backpacking trips. Before fording a stream, I wondered how much chance there was of losing my balance and drowning. At night my anxious mind wrote suspense novels about bear attacks and falling trees. But now, having been to the wilderness and back many times, my fears have been transformed into a heightened state of awareness, where my own instincts lead the way.

The ultralight backpacking philosophy has a unique perspective on the whole notion of safety in the wilderness. Since one of the pillars of going ultralight is to remove the barriers between our everyday lives and the natural world around us, we want to leave behind as much baggage—both physical and mental—as possible. That means we don't carry the fattest first-aid kit available, nor do we take the things that some backpackers insist they need: mace spray, a food canister to foil bears, a GPS unit, a whistle, sometimes even a handgun—the list can go on forever. Instead, we bring the greatest asset we have when the goal is to remain safe, healthy, and content: our minds, and plain old common sense.

Sometimes, our greatest threat to safety isn't what's out there, but rather what's in here, inside our bodies and minds. When people leave home to travel, they seem to become dumber. In Breckenridge, where I worked as a ski instructor, we called the tourists "gapers," because they would become so distracted by the million different things calling for their attention that they would commit the most nonsensical acts. So, part of staying safe in the wilderness is employing some important practices that eventually train our minds to stay focused and aware of our surroundings; stretching, good hygiene, and paying close attention to our senses are but a few.

When I began taking flying lessons, my instructor gave me some advice I've always remembered. "If something doesn't feel right," he said, "then it most likely isn't." Very simply, trust your instincts. If you've got a nagging feeling about something, whether it's the weather or the terrain or any other aspect of your adventure, listen to that voice and make the appropriate changes to correct whatever feels wrong.

Let's spend some time looking at dangers you might encounter in the wilderness and find out how ultralight backpacking can reduce each one to a level where we can be comfortable and safe.

ANIMALS

Contrary to popular belief, bears rampaging through your campsite and mountain lions launching themselves at your chest are events that simply do not happen. Yes, there are isolated incidents, but the biggest threat from wild animals rarely exceeds the occasional mosquito bite. Almost all animals use aggression only as a last resort. It takes but one or two trips into the wilderness to realize there

is little to fear, especially when armed with a little wisdom on how to blend in with nature.

It's not hard to reach a point of mutual respect for the animals you encounter. In fact, some of your most rewarding experiences can come from close contact with wildlife. I remember hiking in the San Felipe Hills of the southern California desert on a cold and rainy day. Rounding another turn on my way up a never-ending string of switchbacks, I stopped dead in my tracks. Immediately before me on the trail, not six feet away, was a gray fox. It stood motionless for perhaps three or four seconds as we locked gazes, seemingly acknowledging each other's rightful presence in these remote hills. And then it darted up the hill with barely a sound. I can still picture that fox's expression. It was not one of fear or of being threatened, but rather one that demonstrated how nature intended two animals to communicate. It reminded me that we don't have to let fear make our decisions for us and that a healthy mutual respect goes a long way.

The particular types of animals that you encounter will depend greatly on where you'll be hiking, and will determine what kind of protection, if any, you need to bring. As in countless other situations, your best protection is ultimately your own brain rather than any sort of material device. Let's first deal with the animal that concerns folks the most—the bear.

Bears

I've spent countless nights in bear country, and to this day have encountered only one who thought my tent looked like a refrigerator—and that was because I stayed at an extremely popular Yosemite campground instead of finding my own site in the back-country. Bears are often conditioned to wandering through places where people have established themselves. If you can find a campsite for yourself away from trails, campgrounds, parking lots, and other well-traveled areas, your chances of encountering a bear are greatly reduced. One strategy that helps minimize bear encounters is to cook your meals and clean up before you reach your campsite. Cooking smells will then be kept away from your actual overnight site.

The usual advice is to hang your food bag from a tree to protect it from bears. This can be a laborious process that bears manage to foil regularly unless you employ an elaborate suspension system. The bag called the Ursack offers an alternative. The Ursack is a pliable bag that looks like a stuff sack, but is made of extremely tough aramid fibers. It weighs less than 4 ounces and can be secured to a tree with the included 5-foot-long super-strength cord. But even this bag and its high-tech cord have been known to eventually give way to bears' efforts in areas where they are more aggressive.

Many backpackers would exile me for saying this, but I often sleep with my food right by my side. I don't want a clever bear to snag my food bag from a tree and leave me with nothing to eat—and the only time a bear came by my tent, I managed to shout him away. But let me hasten to say that I employ certain safeguards: I cook dinner away from my sleeping site; I stay away from popular camping sites; and I put my food in doubled zippered plastic bags.

Important: This tactic of sleeping with food in the tent is reasonable only in areas that bears are known to not frequent. In heavily traveled areas, black bears are becoming more and more aggressive, and under no circumstances would I sleep with food in these places. Practically all of Yosemite and Sequoia National Parks fall into this category. I hardly backpack in Yosemite anymore because I don't want to lug around a protective food box and I don't like staying at those loud, sprawling campsites where reinforced bear boxes offer the only hope of having any food left in the morning.

Use extreme caution in grizzly country. Grizzlies are a lot less demure than black bears.

Smaller Animals

Don't underestimate the resourcefulness and tenacity of badgers, raccoons, marmots, squirrels, and other assorted creatures in getting at your food. Wild animal species have survived for eons by searching for food. But they also recognize someone higher up the food chain, and that's where we have the advantage. Faced with the prospect of going head-on with a human, animals seem to understand that it's best to move on to an easier target.

Use some of the same tricks you would employ with bears. Cook away from your tent, clean up afterward, package the food and store it in a way that makes it difficult for animals to reach the food or to get inside. And keep a close eye on your food sack to spot any creature who tries to burrow into it. (For special cautions in bear country, see the preceding section.)

Mosquitoes

Mosquitoes are renowned for their ability to turn an otherwise pleasant trip into a hysterical slapfest. I suggest never wearing shorts or a short-sleeved shirt while backpacking in mosquito country. The main reason is to save weight, so you don't have to carry both long and short pants and both long-sleeve and short-sleeve shirts. But this is also an effective anti-mosquito strategy. If the area is bug-free and the day is warm, I just pull up the sleeves of my lightweight Capilene top. When mosquitoes launch an offense, I only need to pull down my sleeves and have some protection.

It's true that mosquitoes can bite through clothing, but you'll fare a lot better than with bare skin. Mosquitoes seem to be less attracted to brighter-color clothing, so I wear a white shirt in mosquito-ridden areas.

Always carry a small amount of mosquito repellent that contains the highly effective chemical DEET. Don't get carried away and haul along a gallon of the stuff; small amounts work very well. Finally, keep moving as much as possible since moving targets are harder to nail than stationary ones.

STAYING FOUND

It's easy to say in the safety and comfort of home that getting lost on a backpacking trip is not something that could ever happen. But wait until you're stuck in a thunderstorm and you can't tell where the trail is, your map is soaking wet, and all you want to do is get someplace dry and have something to eat. That's when mistakes happen. It's vital that you always know where you are—and that you remain calm no matter what the circumstances. The only time panicking helps is when . . . well, actually, it never helps.

Bring a map and a good compass and, please, know how to use them. If you aren't familiar with land navigation, read a book, take a class, or have someone show you how to use these lifesaving tools. If I'm headed into a place I already know intimately and it's not that far from a phone or a town, I don't mind leaving map and compass at home to save weight. But if the terrain is even slightly unfamiliar, I will not hesitate to bring an up-to-date map and an orienteering compass.

If you have the time, read a survival manual to help prepare for the worst-case scenario of getting completely lost. You'll find hundreds of survival techniques that could someday save your life. Such a handbook can teach you how to build a shelter, signal for help, trap animals for food, navigate using natural markers, and so on.

WEATHER

Considering the weather before venturing into the backcountry is of paramount importance. If you head out in severe conditions without proper preparation, you could join a long list of people who paid the ultimate price. Use all available resources to determine what you might be in for.

Also be aware that actual conditions could be far different than what you were led to expect. As I prepared for a backpacking trip to the desert one summer, I heard repeated warnings of how the temperatures could rise to above 100°F. On the second day

Wet weather doesn't have to be a deterrent as long as you come prepared.

knows" with everything we did in life, we'd never leave home. Do some research on your destination's climate to give you a sound idea of what kind of protection is appropriate. Then you'll be able to bring the lightest possible gear while still making sure you are covered in case the weather turns foul. And use your common sense, always your best weight-saving tool.

Staying Warm

No matter the season or destination, I bring enough clothes to ensure that I can stay warm in the event that the temperature drops to freezing. Staying warm during colder temperatures is an elemental part not only of surviving, but also of maintaining a positive frame of mind. Not many people find it enjoyable to hunch over a stove, shivering and shaking, vainly trying to rub some heat into their blue hands.

The minimum clothing list for any trip includes long underwear, nylon pants, a fleece top, a rain jacket, and a fleece hat and gloves. The only item I would leave at home if I am as sure as I can be that the days and nights will be mild is the pair of gloves. Don't try to save weight by leaving any of these other items at home. Our weight-saving techniques come from using the lightest possible items that can still carry out their life-sustaining function.

Your body also needs fuel to keep warm. It's as simple as that. If you haven't fed and hydrated your body properly, it's not going to have the resources to generate heat. Once you go down that road, it's a long, hard struggle back to a healthy 98.6°. In a cold environment, it's absolutely crucial that you

of the trip, I awoke to freezing, blowing rain that made me thankful that I had brought enough layers to keep warm.

Ultralight backpacking relies heavily on your common sense. If you're going to the San Bernardino Mountains in southern California in August, you won't carry an arctic sleeping bag. And if it rains half an inch a year where you're going, you don't need a Gore-Tex rain suit. But after all, who knows—the worst could happen. Well, if we said "who

Keep warm by donning layers, eating hot meals, and huddling together if you're with other hikers.

eat and drink regularly so that your body has the fuel it needs to keep you warm.

Let's review the tactics you can use to help stay warm at night:

- Eat hot, protein-laden foods. Try to eat immediately before getting into your sleeping bag, which will make your body produce considerably more heat during the night.

- Empty your bladder before going to bed, thus relieving your body of the need to keep that extra liquid at 98.6°F.

- Spend a few minutes doing jumping jacks or some other blood-pumping exercise.

Doing a few cardiovascular exercises before getting into your bag will help to ensure a warm night.

- Line the inside of your sleeping bag with clothes. You'll be reducing the space inside the bag that your body must heat up, while adding more air pockets to trap warm air.

- Wear a warm hat.

Staying Cool

As important as staying warm on cold days is staying cool on hot days. Water is the main ingredient in a happy hot-weather backpacking experience. As long as you keep yourself sufficiently hydrated, everything else is pretty manageable.

Water bladders, with their accessible hoses hanging off of one shoulder, are far better at keeping you adequately hydrated than water bottles. The hypothetical ideal to keeping hydrated would be to have a constant, uninterrupted flow of water into your body at a rate that exactly compensates for your body's loss of water. Realistically, you'd be hard-pressed to keep the bladder's hose in your mouth all the time, taking small sips with every breath.

The next best thing is to take small sips as often as possible, throughout the day. At least every five minutes, you should take a draw off the hose. You don't need to take huge gulps every time (in fact, you shouldn't); a mouthful or two is sufficient. Believe it or not, you'll actually end up drinking less water by volume than if you were using water bottles and drank only at rest stops, because you're hydrating yourself before your thirst instinct kicks in. If you wait until you actually feel thirsty, you're already well on your way to being dehydrated, and then you end up

Frequent drinks from your water hose is your best defense against dehydration.

drinking more than your body actually needs.

One of the best ways of ensuring that you are keeping yourself adequately hydrated is to monitor the color of your urine. It should be clear and copious; if it is an amber yellow, then you know you need to drink more, and more often.

THE ULTRALIGHT WAY: The Right Amount of Water

It's essential to carry enough water, but you don't want to be laden with water you don't need. That's the problem with water—it's the most essential item in your pack, yet it's also the heaviest. Carrying the right amount—not so little that you become dehydrated, and not so much that you defeat all the ultralight efforts you've made—is a delicate balance that relies on research and experience.

The factors you have to consider when deciding how much water you need are terrain, temperature, how fast you walk, distance between water resupply points, and your general water consumption rate. If I know it's a relatively flat 8 miles between water sources and the day is shaping up to be a scorcher, I know I should be carrying about 2 liters of water when I leave the first water source.

That calculation includes "camelling up" at that first water source—gorging myself on as much water as I can drink while it's available in an unlimited quantity. With this kind of rough calculation, I am going to add a buffer—maybe an extra half-liter of water just in case.

Hot-weather clothing automatically makes you think of shorts and a T-shirt, which also seems to fit in with wanting to go ultralight. But since you would still be packing your long-sleeved shirt and pants for the evening, the shorts and T-shirt are actually going to add weight and fatten up your pack. I have yet to wear a T-shirt while backpacking, and as for shorts, I had my last sunburn and set of thorny scratches and insect bites on my legs a long time ago. I actually find pants cooler in hot weather, because my legs are shaded beneath the nylon. The only other clothing necessity for high temperatures is a sun hat that covers your head and ears, and preferably your neck as well.

Sunscreen is a must for hot-weather hiking, especially at high altitudes. For average days, only a dollop or two will do, so you don't have to bring the whole container. For scorchers, take along as much as you think you need, plus a little more.

FIRST AID

As with so many of the other topics we've covered, injury prevention and treatment for the ultralight backpacker is a function of resourcefulness, experience, and state of mind much more than it is of available first-aid or emergency equipment. It's not essential to bring along the most complete first-aid kit on the shelf. Ultimately, the best tools you have for treating practically any problem is a sound mind and training. And of these two, a sound mind is still the most valuable asset.

If you spend a lot of time backpacking, I strongly urge you to enroll in a wilderness first-aid class. To become a backpacking instructor, I took a four-day WAFA (Wilderness Advanced First Aid) class, an intensive program designed to give its students a working knowledge of how to deal with emergencies. These courses place far more emphasis

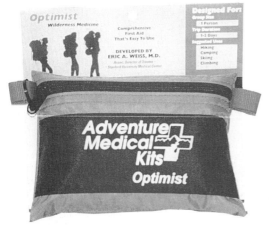

The Optimist, by Adventure Medical Kits.

let provided by Adventure Medical Kits (see appendix) contains a great deal of useful information. As for the first-aid kit itself, you can get by comfortably with a few medications, bandages, disinfectants, and wound dressings (see chapter 6, The Rest of the Gear, for a sample list of contents for a first-aid kit). The most effective help is not going to come from a paramedic-sized first-aid kit, but rather from the effective application of your own resources to an emergency.

on remaining calm and proceeding methodically while stabilizing injuries than on specific medical techniques.

At the least, read a wilderness first-aid manual, or even study the booklet that comes with most wilderness first-aid kits. The book-

DRINKING WATER

We tend to fear things the most when we can't see them. When we look at a mountain stream or lake, our minds may envision teeming legions of invisible parasites and bacteria—despite the fact that a great deal of the water coursing through the moun-

The most important aspect of responding to an emergency in the wilderness is staying calm and focused.

tains is as pure and potable as any found on earth. We've been trained to think that every last ounce of water must be cleaned to prepare it for our sensitive bodies.

To play it safe, I certainly advise treating the water you drink. But I'll also mention that I've drunk natural water straight from the source many times and have never become ill.

There are three main groups of uglies that we are concerned with. The largest in size come in the form of cysts, including the dreaded *Giardia lamblia*. Giardiasis, the illness resulting from ingesting giardia, can be pretty vicious, with diarrhea, cramps, fever, and other symptoms. *Cryptosporidium* is another nasty cyst parasite. The next size down are bacteria, the most notable of which is *E. coli*. The smallest organisms are viruses.

To make water potable, you can boil, filter, or chemically treat it. No single approach offers the perfect solution. Boiling the water is the most effective method, but also the least practical. Modern water filters will remove all these organisms except for viruses. However, waterborne viruses are extremely rare in the Western world.

Iodine and chlorine tablets can kill most organisms (but not always as cysts) in tainted water, but you have to wait about half an hour before purification is complete (an hour or more if the water is very cold), and it leaves the water with an unpleasant taste.

HYGIENE

With all the luxuries now available in domestic hygiene, I can say unequivocally that your hygienic practices in the wilderness will have to be brought down a couple notches. That's

Fill your pot with water and use your hand towel to bathe.

not to say you can't be clean; it's just that you may have to revise your definition of clean to mean somewhat better than filthy. As you backpack, you will become intimately familiar with odors you had no idea your body could produce. A proper shower, when you are finally able to take one, will feel like heaven itself.

Backpackers have the option of hauling along all kinds of hygienic paraphernalia, from skin softening cream with aloe to sticks of deodorant to bottles of perfume shaped like the Venus de Milo. My particular favorite example of extravagant backcountry hygiene is the backpacking shower. Some of these devices are so elaborate that I have to wonder if their users didn't pull out the plumbing from their home showers and pack it along with them.

Ultralight backpackers proudly shun such trivial luxury and instead get by with a toothbrush sawed in half, a bit of tooth powder, and a small bottle of liquid soap. That's all you need to keep yourself hygienically safe.

If you want to give yourself a rugged version of a bath, use a pot of water with your hand towel and a bit of liquid soap to wash your body. Bathe a good distance from any natural source of water. Dispose of the soapy water by pouring it into a sinkhole that you've dug at least six inches deep. Use as little soap as possible.

STRETCHING

Ask any group of yoga aficionados if stretching is important, and they will react as if you had asked them if the earth is indeed round. Yes, stretching is vital.

A simple stretching regimen takes only about five minutes, yet can prevent years of musculoskeletal-related injuries. Stretching allows you to recruit the maximum utility of a muscle while keeping it relaxed and free of stress-induced soreness. I stretch just before I start hiking each morning, and then about once an hour for the rest of the day. Right before I go to sleep for the night, I stretch everything again. I spend more time on the morning and evening stretches, holding each position for a little longer than while I'm on the trail.

I follow the same basic exercises, moving from larger muscles to smaller ones. Following is a simple stretching regimen that takes only a few minutes to perform. Hold each stretch for a count of ten (using the one-one-thousand, two-one-thousand method). Each

> # THE ULTRALIGHT WAY:
> ## GOING NATURAL
>
> It's up to you how meticulous you want to be with your hygiene. I'll admit without my cheeks turning red that my level of hygiene is what I like to call "natural." The only time I really use soap on a regular basis is when I heed the principal rule of backcountry hygiene: Wash your hands before handling food. This is an absolute imperative, and there are no exceptions.
>
> There's nothing inherently wrong with getting dirty and smelling foul, as long as it doesn't interfere with your basic health. It's the way humans lived for a long, long time, and it allows us to appreciate, rather than take for granted, the comforts and luxuries of home.

stretch is done twice, one for each side of the body.

1. Balance yourself and stretch your quads (the muscles on the front of the thigh) by holding your foot and pressing it against your buttocks while keeping your thigh perpendicular to the ground.

2. Cross one foot in front of the other and reach down toward the ground to stretch the hamstrings (the muscles on the back of the thigh).

3. Rest the heel of your straightened leg on something stable at about waist level. Keep your knee as straight as you can as you bend down toward your foot.

The calf stretch.

4. Push your hands against a tree or a wall, with your body at a 30-degree angle to the ground (see photo above). Put one foot in front of the other, and press your rear heel down to the ground to stretch the calves. (You can accomplish this same stretch by resting the ball of your foot on a ledge while holding yourself steady, and gently pressing your heel down.)

5. If you are familiar with yoga, you'll appreciate one of my favorite stretches, the knee-down twist (see photo, next page). Lie on your back and press your left palm on the outside of your raised right knee. Press that knee down to the ground on your left side while extending your right arm straight out from your body, letting the arm rest on the ground. Now look at your right hand and breathe deeply, feeling your spine and the muscles of your lower back flow with pleasure. Hold for a few deep breaths, and do the same stretch for the other side.

In the morning, I like to add a simple torso rotation. Rotate your torso back and forth a few times while standing erect to

The knee-down twist is an effective yoga stretch.

loosen up the muscles that will keep you steady as you walk with the pack. Add a couple of arm rotations and you're primed and ready to hit the trail.

If you have experience with yoga, feel free to incorporate as many stretches as you like into your own personalized stretching regimen. If you've never engaged in yoga, I strongly urge you to take a class and give it

a chance. Yoga has worked nothing short of miracles for my body (which had always been stiff and unyielding) and mind.

I also like to massage my feet right before I go to sleep. I spend about five minutes rubbing the muscles and tissue, paying special attention to the soles. I can't say whether there is any physiological benefit, but it feels just too darned good to give up.

CHAPTER 9
WALKING

YOU MAY WONDER WHAT THERE IS TO discuss in a chapter on the subject of walking. After all, you've been walking almost all your life without much trouble or effort, so what's the purpose of devoting an entire chapter to something so natural?

In answering that question, consider how efficiently your foot has been designed to perform the natural task of making contact with the earth. As we saw in the chapter on footwear, the complex mechanism of the foot evolved as a way to support our weight and propel us forward. Shoes weren't part of the equation.

In ultralight backpacking, our aim is to use our natural physical resources in the most efficient manner possible. Yet we have been constantly trained to deny the foot its inherent powers by trapping it within a hard shell. When we tossed away those concrete blocks called hiking boots and donned lightweight trail shoes, we gave back to the foot its ability to perform economically and naturally. And with that comes an opportunity

for us to learn to walk more efficiently to take full advantage of our liberated feet.

Ultralight backpacking has a lot to do with efficiency. In terms of walking, efficiency is being able to walk as far as possible with the least amount of work. On the smallest scale, we want to expend the least amount of energy to transfer our weight from one foot to the other as we take each step.

In our culture of motorized transportation, there's little need to walk with efficiency. We don't walk, we drive—even if it's just to the grocery store around the corner. If I told you that the movie you were waiting for was playing at a theater 10 miles away, the idea of walking there would seem absurd. But the wilderness changes our priorities. If we were in the heart of Yosemite, surrounded by towering walls of granite and rolling meadows of wildflowers, and I told you of a spectacular lake 10 miles away, you might just be charging down the trail before I even finished telling you about it. A mile is a mile whether you're in Yosemite or downtown, but environment and intention cast each one in a very different light.

Before leaving for the Pacific Crest Trail, I remember trying to grasp the concept of 20 miles in a single day by driving my car that far, over and over. But of course I was driving on a suburban road, surrounded by burger marts and gas stations, so I couldn't really appreciate what it would mean to hike 20 miles every day in a place without so much as an electrical plug for 50 miles. Once I was on the trail, surrounded by nature on all sides and nothing but the next hill or valley marking my distance, I averaged 21 miles a day for 250 miles. Something changed within me the moment I left the trappings of civilization and cloaked myself in the pure air of nature. My body and my spirit felt a deep sense of confidence and release. It was like coming home.

Prehistoric humans had to use mind and body in the most efficient way possible; it meant the difference between survival and extinction. That mental mode of efficiency is so deeply rooted that even today, our brains automatically undergo a transformation when we set foot into the wilderness. Now, let's integrate a little guidance along with the instincts you already have, so that your body can follow the intuitive wishes of your mind.

RELAXATION: THE STRONGEST MUSCLE

In order for us to walk efficiently, we first need to become familiar with our own bodies. At home, with your shoes and socks off, practice taking steps very, very slowly. Feel every muscle contract and expand as your body moves from one step to the next. Close your eyes when trying this exercise; you can hold onto something for balance.

Keep your knees slightly bent the whole time. Feel the tension in your thigh and calf as each foot reaches forward. Feel the final thrust as your rear foot leaves the ground. Finally, feel the relaxation of your leg muscles as the leg moves forward to plant the beginning of the next step. It's that sense of relaxation that we want to develop.

As you become more familiar with which muscles propel you forward, start looking for ways of cutting down on the energy needed to take that next step. Experiment with the relative placement of your hips over your legs. Try to keep your hips perfectly centered. Right in the middle of your hip cavity is the magical spot known as your center of gravity. Everything else spreads out from this spot. Call it the Continental Divide of your body.

When you throw on a backpack, you raise your center of gravity, making you more top-heavy. Therefore, it is crucial that you center your hips over your legs so that they can support your torso in the most efficient manner possible. If, instead, you move your hips around, then your leg, abdominal, and lower back muscles must strain to keep your center of gravity from exceeding its envelope. And what happens when that magical spot breaks the envelope? The floor will turn into your best friend, because you'll be hugging it.

As you start to get a clear picture of how your body actually takes a step, pick up the pace a little. Find an open space where you can walk with your eyes closed, shutting out distractions. Feel how your arms complement your legs by counterbalancing their movements. Focus on keeping your chest pointing in the direction you are moving. Keep your head level and stable. Continue being aware of every muscle's contraction and then its relaxation, trying to use each one as slightly as possible. Fully extend your spine by imagining someone pulling a string attached to the top of your head.

By opening up your mind to your own body, you are in fact turning the subconscious into the conscious. That is the only way to retrain yourself. Once you consciously practice walking the correct way, this knowledge will slowly turn back into being a subconscious action.

As you practice walking, try to imagine that your muscles don't do anything unless you give them a command. With every motion, visualize giving the green light to every muscle that is a part of that particular motion. If some errant muscle slips by without you consciously giving it a command, make sure it doesn't get away with that again. At first, you will probably find this exercise difficult. But as you become more intimate with your body, you'll feel muscles and tissue you never even knew existed.

The next exercise is to consciously allow your muscles to relax as much as possible. As soon as each muscle's job is over, it should instantly become relaxed until it is needed again.

Again, start slowly, and concentrate on using each muscle only when it is needed. Find some stairs and practice walking up and down. By the time each foot leaves the ground, the same leg should be as relaxed as possible. Once you start moving faster, your own momentum will allow each leg to relax even more as it reaches for the next step. By relaxing your muscles, you are allowing oxygen and blood to circulate more freely through them, carrying away lactic acid and increasing their stamina.

BONES: THE SOFT TOUCH

Let's now shift from the muscles to another part of your body that needs a lot of respect if you want it to treat you nicely: your skeleton. Bones take much longer than muscles to show signs of abuse. Muscles react quickly to your behavior, and they will let you know if you've been disrespectful to them. But even if you slam your feet down hard enough to jar your teeth right out of your skull, your bones will probably hold up for a long time.

If you keep that kind of abuse up, however, your bones will punish you far worse than any muscle in the long run. Even though there may not be any such thing as sore bones, we still need to treat them with as much respect as we do our muscles.

The most important way of taking care of our skeletal structure is to be gentle to it. Place each foot down as softly as you can. Think of a cat and how it appears to place its paws down carefully and gently with each step. This is where light, flexible shoes come into play. With heavy, stiff boots, it's much harder to land each foot gently than it is with the shoes you're wearing as an ultralight backpacker.

Your heel should be the first part of the foot to touch the earth, smoothly transitioning all the way up to the toes. Move your body weight fluidly through the length of the foot, from heel to big toe. Imagine that the ground is very delicate, and that you must make as little impression upon its surface as you can.

KEEPING PACE

Now that you've practiced walking on a very conscious level, let's broaden the picture a bit. How fast or slowly should you link your steps? What is your most efficient hiking speed?

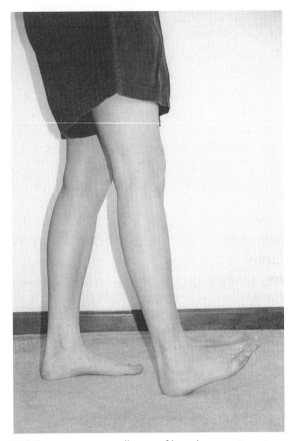

While practicing walking softly, take your time to feel every nuance of your step. The best way of doing this is barefoot, with eyes closed and holding onto something for balance.

Finding your own most efficient pace depends on what you're trying to achieve. An efficient pace for a sprinter is one that maintains the highest possible speed for about 10 seconds. For an ultralight backpacker, speed is not as much of a factor. As a matter of fact, the faster you walk, the more sloppy and less efficient you become. By trying to keep up a fast pace, you burn a lot of energy and tire yourself more quickly than if you were walking slowly. The answer is not to walk faster, but to walk for a longer period of time.

To get the most out of the hiking day, rise early. I usually get up at around 6:00 or 6:30; some people get up as early as 4:00. After you rise, get on the trail as soon as you can. I break camp as soon as I'm up, and I'll eat a granola bar as I start walking. It takes me a little under half an hour between opening my eyes and taking the day's first step on the trail. If you plan on hiking 20 miles, allow yourself a full 12 hours.

The most important piece of advice I can give you in this chapter is to walk at a comfortable pace. I know that sounds vague, but I'm really speaking in specific terms. A comfortable pace is the pace at which you aren't exerting yourself beyond what it takes to walk with the tools of efficiency that we've been discussing. Walk slowly enough that you aren't panting and can breathe through your nose.

Backpacking is all about endurance rather than brute strength, and there is a cardiovascular point where your body can maintain a level of activity almost indefinitely. In theory, the only reasons you would ever stop walking is that you've reached your destination, you need to refuel your body, or you need to go to the bathroom. You should never have to stop hiking because you're exhausted or your muscles hurt too much to go on.

At the right pace, you could conceivably walk thousands of miles without ever having to stop except to sleep. And that's exactly how people are able to hike long distances—they have found their most efficient pace, and they are able to maintain it day after day for months.

The right pace is usually a lot slower than you might expect. When I take my backpacking students out on trips, we walk very slowly, and inevitably someone asks why we're making like snails. Sometimes, if they ask more than once, I'll have them carry an extra 10 pounds and then they usually stop asking. But otherwise, I explain that we want to keep our muscles and circulatory system fresh and ready for the next day after a good night's sleep. I could take that thought even further and say that we want them to be fresh and ready for even the next *step*. It's the classic tortoise-and-hare story, in a backpacking context.

To be sure you reach your campsite before dark, use planning instead of extra speed to make it on time. Plan out your route in the morning so you don't arrive at the base of a 3,000-foot-hill at five in the afternoon. Slogging up endless switchbacks can be exhausting and aggravating, but it doesn't have to be. Going uphill is where pacing becomes most important. Goooo slooooow.

REST BREAKS

Once you find an ideal pace, you might be able to just keep on walking until the sun goes down. But taking breaks at the right time and in the right manner is an important part of your day, especially on a trip that is longer than three or four days. Breaks provide a brief respite for your muscles to relax, and give you a chance to stretch, nibble on a snack, or absorb the view.

Try to limit your breaks to no longer than 10 minutes, so that your muscles don't go into ultra-relaxed mode and perform only reluctantly when you're ready to move on.

Take breaks often, making sure that your feet are slightly elevated. This is also a good time to eat a snack, rehydrate, or just enjoy the view.

If you want to have a lunch break in the middle of the day, a single half-hour stop is acceptable.

Take your breaks once every hour. Sometimes an hour will fly by and you may want to just keep walking, but take the break anyway. It's all part of treating your body efficiently. However, feel free to employ your own strategy for breaks as circumstances dictate. When I head out and I know I'll be hiking about 10 to 15 miles over the course of the day, I like to get up early and begin by hiking a solid two hours before taking a break. That way, I've covered at least a third of the entire day's hiking by nine o'clock or so. I never want to feel in a rush, so I try to cover the most miles in the morning, leaving the rest of the day to take it easy.

When you take your breaks, sit so that you feet are slightly elevated. Otherwise, your blood will pool toward your feet and your muscles won't function efficiently once you start walking again.

TREKKING POLES

At last we arrive at the subject of one of the most heated debates among backpackers. To pole or not to pole? First, let me tell you my experience with trekking poles. I started out backpacking with no poles, thinking they were just for skiers or for people with exceptionally bad balance. Occasionally on the trail I'd hear the clickety-clack of be-poled backpackers rounding the corner, and I'd ask them how they liked the poles. After several people told me they would never backpack again without them, I decided to give them a try. And now it's my turn to tell you that I'd never backpack without them.

The advantages of poles are numerous, but I'll start off with the most compelling one. Every time you plant a pole, you apply about 10 pounds of pressure to it. That's 10 pounds per step that your legs and feet don't have to bear. As far as your feet are concerned, you weigh 10 pounds less.

The benefits don't just stop there. Poles give you two extra points of balance. When crossing streams or walking over uneven terrain, you'll be darn glad you've got those poles to keep yourself balanced. Although I wouldn't advise this, I've crossed steep snow fields with just my poles for balance when an ice ax wasn't handy.

Poles also provide your arms and upper body with a workout. You can use them as supports for a tarp. And walking with poles makes it a lot easier to develop a rhythmic walking pace. Try it and you'll see what I mean.

There are, of course, some disadvantages that I should point out. Poles obviously weigh something, so you have to assess that extra weight against their value to you. Poles can get caught up in bushes. And pole tips are usually made with a hard material, like carbide, that leaves pockmarks in the ground. I put plastic or rubber tips on the ends to minimize their impact on the ground.

I've hiked extensively both with poles and

Trekking poles help you keep your balance and take the weight off of your feet. They are especially useful in fording a stream.

THE ULTRALIGHT WAY: How to Breathe

You can improve the efficiency of your breathing while hiking, as while walking. Inefficient breathing may not affect you that much as you wait in line at the bank, but when you're backpacking or swimming or rock climbing, correct breathing is vital.

From breathing comes everything else. I didn't realize the importance of efficient breathing until I started yoga practice and combined its emphasis on deep, conscious breathing with my backpacking. It immediately made a huge difference. It soon felt as if breathing was the glue that held together every part of the backpacking experience. In fact, incorporating my breathing practice into backpacking brought me into a deeper appreciation for nature and for the way I interacted with it. I had something of a revelation; it all starts with breathing.

Before you begin practicing conscious breathing on the trail, a good idea is to start at home where you can first grasp the concept. Start by making yourself comfortable in a quiet and pleasant space. You can sit on the floor or on the lawn with your legs crossed in the traditional meditation posture or you can sit in a chair; you can even be standing up. Just be sure your torso is vertical, since this provides you with a natural breathing posture.

Now, breathe slowly and deeply, letting your own natural forces dictate each breath as much as possible. The goal is to become conscious and aware of your breathing without consciously taking it over. Let it occur naturally, fully sensing and feeling every inhalation and every exhalation. Focus only on your breathing, listening for its rhythm.

As you go about your day, keep trying to focus on your breathing. Each breath should be full, taking advantage of your entire lung's capacity. You may find yourself feeling more relaxed and comfortable almost immediately.

Once you get the hang of it, get out on the trail and practice your conscious breathing there. You should begin feeling better right away. Feel your breath as it spreads through every part of your body, carrying vital oxygen to all muscles and tissue.

There's a purity and simplicity about deep breathing that represents what we're striving to achieve in ultralight backpacking. Take the time to get closer to your breathing. Make it deep, full, and aware. Just like becoming an ultralight backpacker, efficient breathing takes practice and discipline. And eventually, you'll do it naturally.

without, and for me, the benefits of poles far exceed their drawbacks. More and more people are using them now, and there's much less chance that someone will make fun of you and ask where the nearest ski run is. Along with lightweight trail shoes, trekking poles have made the biggest difference in my backpacking.

My favorite brand of trekking pole is Leki. The company offers a line of ultralight telescoping poles, called Ultralite Ti, that incorporate thinner shaft diameters and lighter-weight alloys than most other poles. They have comfortable cork or rubberized grips, and some incorporate a spring-assisted antishock feature.

CHAPTER 10

THE ULTRALIGHT STATE OF MIND

AFTER ALL THE DISCUSSIONS OF packweight, materials, and ultralight techniques, there remains the subject that is the foundation for everything else. What is the purpose, the real driving purpose, of ultralight backpacking? Sure, on the surface you get a lighter pack and the ability to walk farther with less physical exertion. But what is making all that happen? Why is the practice of ultralight backpacking closer to the ideal way in which to spend time in nature? I'd like to delve a bit deeper into these questions and talk about the state of mind we are striving for whenever we step into the wilderness.

THE MOST ESSENTIAL PIECE OF GEAR

One piece of gear far outweighs everything else in value and utility. That piece of gear is, of course, your own mind. After spending so much time lightening our packs, shelter, clothing, and everything else that we take

into the backcountry, we often forget that there is still that one vitally important part of us that can also use some lightening up. The mind is very much a part of the ultralight method, and we need to apply ultralight techniques to it as well.

You had everything you needed to be an ultralight backpacker before you even picked this book up. At the heart of things, ultralight backpacking is a state of mind. All of the information on packs and tents and sleeping bags is irrelevant if there's not this particular consciousness to hold it all together.

Try for a moment to forget everything you have ever learned—all the classes you ever took, the books you ever read, the late-night conversations you ever had. This state of mind where we forget everything else is what we strive to attain in ultralight backpacking. When we simplify everything to its most rudimentary form, when all that matters is breathing and being aware of our existence, what we find is a sudden realization that our existence is a part of something much greater.

It is at this crucial point that we feel pulled toward the places where we can be in this state of mind as deeply as possible.

The place could be the John Muir Wilderness in the California Sierras, or on top of Mount Washington in New Hampshire, or along the Rio Grande in Big Bend National Park in Texas. Such places are all connected in their complete and utmost simplicity of being, and our awareness of that simplicity is why we are so drawn to them.

THE MYTHOLOGY OF GEAR

Throughout this book, I've tried to emphasize that no piece of manufactured gear is absolutely essential in determining the outcome of a backpacking experience. You don't want to rely on something external for your ultimate safety or well-being. But when you consider how unpredictable we have always believed nature to be, you can see how a massive overemphasis on gear came to govern the world of backpacking.

The old school of thought would have you believe that you'd be a fool to take on nature without arming yourself with every conceivable measure of safety and comfort under the sun. But that isn't what being in nature is all about. Rather, it's about feeling free, unbounded, shedding the distractions and barriers of our civilization—not bringing them with us.

The perception that gear is all-important is sometimes a sign of how effective marketers are at exploiting our fears. For example, people are afraid of bears attacking them, so a company recognizes a potentially huge market and makes a spray that is supposed to repel any attacking bear. Spraying a small can of mace into a bear's face would probably do little more than provide you with an extremely rare glimpse of a bear doubled over in laughter. But plenty of people buy this spray and then set off into bear country thinking they are now invincible. The spray gives them a false sense of security that could place them in more danger than before.

FROM EQUIPMENT RELIANCE TO SELF-RELIANCE

The transition from relying on gear to relying on yourself is central to your growth as an ultralight backpacker. Such a transition brings together all the elements of this entire book. We are so accustomed to relying on the mechanisms that we've devised to make life easier that the ability to know and rely on ourselves seems to occupy a distant horizon. But this ability lives within us all, waiting like a light to come on. We just don't know it's there because we've never had to use it.

I'm sure you've heard stories of people who have accomplished great feats of endurance and resourcefulness under extremely trying conditions. It is that deep part of our minds and souls, the part we instinctually tap into at moments of crisis, that we want to adopt as ultralight backpackers. It sometimes takes an intense experience to awaken that part of us, but through practice and discipline, we can attain that state of mind in our daily lives.

In the ultralight state of mind, we let our deepest instincts take over as much as possible. The oft-heard saying that "your instincts are never wrong" has a lot of truth to it. But in our everyday busy lives, it's difficult to separate instinct from the way we've been conditioned to behave after a lifetime's exposure to modern civilization. In nature, where gravity is the only law and survival the only rule, our instincts can be let free to take their most natural course.

To free our instincts, we have to consciously shed the things that keep them trapped. That's what many of us are afraid of when our thoughts turn to the wilderness. And that's why we bring so much stuff with us—to stave off the feelings of fear associated with becoming naked and letting our instincts take over. This is precisely what ultralight backpacking addresses—making it easier for us to shed the things that trap our instincts.

Nature isn't just out there, beyond the city limits and away from buildings and roads. We are nature ourselves, and going ultralight gives us a way to connect the nature in here with the nature out there—and to do it neither with fear nor with the walls our fear erects.

MEDITATION

In daily life, there is precious little time to let our minds rest quietly. Our brains are so used to being fed a constant diet of stimulation that we find it difficult to engage in the practice of doing nothing. The interesting thing about cutting off that stimulation for

Becoming more aware of your mind and body through meditation can bring you into a much deeper connection with nature and is an integral part of adopting the philosophy and essence of ultralight backpacking.

a little while is what remains behind. Rather than our minds being left an empty box, they become conduits for the myriad thoughts, emotions, and cerebrations that never had a chance to flow before. That is one of the gifts of meditation.

You can practice meditation anywhere, at any time—sitting in your car at a red light, eating dinner in a restaurant, and yes, backpacking along a trail. The most profound meditative states I've ever reached came while walking by myself along a trail deep in the backcountry, immersed completely in the world around me and within my own self. If you want to learn about meditating, check at any bookstore or library for books that can introduce you to the various forms of meditation.

Nature is like one giant meditation room. Whether we are striding along a rugged trail beneath a canopy of dense pine trees, or sitting on a granite rock overlooking a glass-smooth lake, or standing high up on a lonesome peak with a view that stretches into infinity, nature provides us all with an opportunity to turn down the volume of our everyday lives and become utterly connected with who we truly are. I don't think I've ever taken a single trip to the wilderness without coming back feeling more aware of myself and appreciative of the people and the world around me.

Practically all forms of meditation revolve around the breath and the kind of deep, conscious breathing that was discussed in chapter 9, Walking. Everything begins and ends with breathing, and everything is born and dies with breathing. When I walk along the trail, I think about my breath, about taking deep, full inhalations and exhalations. I let the in-breath take in all of the beauty and harmony of nature that surrounds me, and I let out all of my distractions, insecurities, and frustrations in the out-breath.

That's really all there is to it. Even this simple form of meditation won't bring rewards right away, so be patient and set realistic expectations. Better yet, don't have expectations at all. Just let whatever happens, happen. Instead of always trying to reach for something, enjoy wherever you are right now, in this moment. Stay focused, disciplined in your breathing, and everything will come in its time.

WILDERNESS ETHICS

The root of wilderness ethics is responsibility and respect. It sounds simple, but it can be very hard to practice if approached from a negative point of view. It is amazingly easy to say to yourself, "Oh, I'm just one person, what difference could I make?" It's also easy to fall into the trap of wanting to rebel against all the guidelines that wilderness ethics can impose on us. Do I really need to pee 200 feet away from that stream? Who cares if I take this little shortcut so I don't have to walk the entire switchback?

I learned my own lesson in wilderness ethics on a backpacking trip to a remote section of the Sierras. I spent several hours hiking up a beautiful creek, marveling at an endless series of small waterfalls, and found a perfect campsite covered with soft pine needles and shaded by massive sequoia trees. I'm sure you can picture the look of disgust on my face when I found an empty beer bottle lying in the middle of the campsite. Then I

THE ULTRALIGHT WAY: SHARING

Saturday night is a special night for my group of backpacking students. It has been a long day for them, and you can see in their faces a sense of pleasant exhaustion. Many of them have never experienced a night away from a bed and a roof, and they are often overcome with the rapture of the world around them.

After dinner, we sit in a circle, either on logs or on the ground. As we digest our hearty meal, we go around the group and give each person an opportunity to share something that is personally significant.

Some recite poems whose meaning is cast in a new light by the experiences of the day. Someone once read Nelson Mandela's inauguration speech. A student who was a masseuse once gave us all massages. When my turn comes, I always read the same quote from my favorite poem, Walt Whitman's "Song of the Open Road," from *Leaves of Grass*: "Now I see the secret of the making of the best persons, it is to grow in the open air and to eat and sleep with the earth."

Even though we've known one another for only a few hours, everyone opens up a part of themselves that brings us all together in appreciation and intimacy. It seems like each person has left his or her ego somewhere along the trail, and we are all somehow connected, sacred in our place in nature.

How often can you bring together a group of people from different backgrounds and have them share a space for a short time and be so completely open, selfless, and present? I've seen it happen on every one of my trips as an instructor, and I never fail to be awed by it. Nature has that gift to give us, and whether it is through ultralight backpacking or any other outdoor pursuit, it is up to us to accept it.

found the remnants of a campfire that had not been properly set up or extinguished. Cigarette butts littered the area.

That experience showed me why having a wilderness ethic is vital. Nature is a haven, a sanctuary of peace and tranquillity that I want to be able to enjoy for the rest of my life. I want my children to be able to enjoy nature, and their children too. Sharing wilderness ethics is an important step toward ensuring that the wild places will be there for as long as people are around to enjoy them.

Before I take my backpacking class into the backcountry, we spend some time talking about how to be a responsible backpacker. I try to avoid dumping a hundred rules on them without first explaining them and pointing out that nobody is going to enforce them better than the students themselves. Once they understand why we need to make a concerted effort at preserving our natural environment, the rules don't seem like rules anymore and simply become normal, natural behavior.

So I'm not going to list a hundred ways to keep nature natural. If you just remember to be responsible and to respect your surroundings, everything else should become clear.

A good focus for thinking about wilderness responsibility is the Leave No Trace wilderness ethic. The Leave No Trace program was devised to provide standardized principles of minimum-impact camping and hiking. Even though the principles are somebody else's judgment of how the rest of us should behave in the wilderness, many of the ideas on the list would come naturally to anyone who understood why they exist in the first place. The principles include:

Travel and camp on durable surfaces. Look at topo maps and see where suitable campsites exist. Choose campsites according to how little they impact the area. Camp at an established site or on solid rock, rather than in a meadow blossoming with wildflowers. In walking, using your stove, going to the bathroom, and in all activities, look for ways to minimize damage to soil and plants.

Pack it in, pack it out. Everything you bring with you from the trailhead should come back out with you at the end of the trip.

Properly dispose of human waste. Dig a cathole 6 inches deep, and at least 200 feet from any water source. When you've taken care of business, cover up the hole and return the area to its natural state.

Leave what you find. Try to leave the environment as it was when you found it, with no signs of your passage. A few people seem to think that nature is a gift shop, full of souvenirs to take home. Nature is indeed a gift, but the only souvenirs we should take home are memories.

Minimize campfire impact. Campfires scar an area in a sometimes permanent way. The preferred approach is to use your backpacking stove instead. If you do make a campfire, keep it small, use only dead wood, and thoroughly extinguish the fire afterward.

These principles are a recognition that the planet's places of wilderness are dwindling. You probably wouldn't know it as you stand on a high alpine peak, seeing nothing but untouched nature for a hundred miles, but threats to the natural world are very real. Wilderness ethics are a way for you and me, as individuals, to make a positive difference in how our planet will be left to our descendants.

CHAPTER 11
ON THE
LONG-DISTANCE TRAIL

Hiking a long-distance trail is the ultimate pursuit of the ultralight backpacking lifestyle. It is a complete immersion in the natural environment, where the trail becomes a living entity and the trees, mountains, and rivers become your only home. There are a multitude of reasons for hiking a long-distance trail, but practically everyone who completes it will be changed forever.

Among climbers, the ultimate expression of the connection between person and rock is climbing free solo—without ropes, anchors, harnesses, or any other protective device. The only pieces of gear a free soloer needs are climbing shoes and a chalk bag. It takes a certain mind-set to free solo. Free soloists are utterly devoted to the rock, totally confident in every facet of their craft, and intimately familiar with every part of their mind so that fear can never gain a foothold.

Thru-hikers—those hikers who walk from one end of a long-distance trail to the other—have similar mind-sets. Only those

who are committed to immersing themselves in nature and who possess a personal discipline far beyond that of the average person have what it takes to thru-hike a long-distance trail. It takes complete determination, an extremely high level of physical fitness and endurance, inner strength, and a belief in yourself that takes a long time to develop.

You also have to be able to devote half a year to the hike itself in the case of the nation's three best-known routes: the Appalachian Trail (2,100 miles) in the eastern United States; the Pacific Crest Trail (2,600 miles) in the West; and the Continental Divide Trail (3,200 miles), which traces its namesake along the backbone of the Rocky Mountains. And you're looking at more than a year for the America Discovery Trail, which winds more than 6,000 miles coast-to-coast from Washington, D.C., to San Francisco.

Thru-hiking demands intense planning and training. It is during these months prior to a thru-hike attempt that you'll be able to decide if you're actually capable of doing what everyone is undoubtedly calling the craziest thing you've ever come up with.

TRAINING

Training for a long-distance trail involves your mind as much as your body. You'll need to develop a mental discipline that will keep you going, day after day, mile after mile—even state after state. You'll want to spend about six months getting yourself mentally and physically prepared.

Physical training basically involves doing what you'll be doing on the trail, but in a more controlled environment so that you can work on any deficiencies. For example, if you find that your shoulders become sore and fatigued during training hikes, you have the chance to troubleshoot the problem. It could just be a matter of adjusting your pack or getting used to its pressure on your shoulders, or you may need a different pack altogether. At least you'll know exactly what the problem is before starting the thru-hike.

That's mostly what training is all about: letting all the various idiosyncrasies of a long hike present themselves ahead of time so you can address them before you start.

LOGISTICS AND PLANNING

A thru-hike is a major exercise in logistics. You'll need to find a coordinator you can absolutely trust. The coordinator will send out your food packages to resupply points along the route, acquire any equipment you might suddenly need, and generally support you in every way. If a trekking pole breaks, a good logistics coordinator will already know what kind of pole you need and where to get it, and will send it to a place where you can retrieve it as soon as possible.

Spend ample time getting information on resupply points along your trail. If the trail has an associated guidebook, use it to learn about campsites, water sources, and places near the route to obtain supplementary meals and supplies. Each night during your training period, read the equivalent of one day's hiking. Try to envision the trail, picturing the peaks, valleys, and ridges described in the book.

Join the e-mail list for the trail that you will be hiking (see appendix at the back of the book). Post any questions that you might have, and you are sure to receive intelligent and informative responses. Browse through the list's archives, where lots of useful information from past discussion is stored.

MENTAL ADJUSTMENTS

No matter what inspires you to take that first step on a long-distance trail, be prepared for some major mental adjustments. The first big changes come when you start on the trail, while other changes, usually more challenging, can be expected after you get off.

It will take several days, perhaps even a couple of weeks, to become accustomed to life on the trail. The comforts of home will seem enticing, and you may find yourself longing for a familiar world. Then, suddenly, you will feel like you have broken through an invisible wall. Your body, mind, and soul have embraced trail life, and yearnings for your old home trickle away like the last rivulets of snowmelt in spring. This is a wonderful feeling that will charge you with new vigor and energy.

Months later, when you've reached the end of the trail, you face the challenge of having to assimilate back into society. Sure, you could just run off into the mountains and write manifestos for the rest of your life, but you'll probably elect to apply your new experiences to life within your community. You may notice how much faster the world seems to operate than before you left. You'll probably drive 20 miles below the speed limit for a while, and everyone will seem to be in a terrible hurry. This can be a disorienting period, but also one that lets you celebrate your newfound ability to appreciate life at a walking pace.

You will feel many emotions walking a long-distance trail—excitement, surprise, exhaustion, awareness, frustration, complete confidence and a complete lack of it. The best path through this tapestry of emotions is to remain honest with yourself and remember why you began this thru-hike in the first place. Many thru-hikers have completed their own hikes well short of the geographical terminus of the trail because they found whatever it was they set out to seek. Try not to get caught up in the overwhelming nature of a thru-hike; as long as you focus primarily on setting one foot in front of the other, staying in each moment, you will be successful no matter what the outcome.

TRAINING: MONTH-BY-MONTH

During the six-month training period before I made an attempt on the Pacific Crest Trail, I spent most of the time getting my body ready to endure the rigors of trying to hike 2,600 miles. I did everything from lifting weights to running up snow-covered hills. But despite the endless hours of training, I felt intuitively that I could have hiked the trail without ever lifting a single weight or running a single yard. Our bodies are much more capable of physical duress than our minds give them credit for. The physical training certainly helps a great deal in making the hiking easier, but practically all of the training really serves to condition the mind into believing that the body is adequately prepared for being pushed to the limit.

The rest of this chapter lays out a training regimen for the long-distance hiker. However, it can help anyone looking to reach the pinnacle of ultralight backpacking fitness. You can continue with your regular job during the training period, but don't expect to have a lot of free time. Don't allow yourself to miss a single day of training. Adherence to the schedule serves, more than anything, to develop your mental stamina. With this discipline, you can be confident that once you're on the trail, you'll wake each morning with the determination to continue.

I find meditation an invaluable ally, and I'd highly recommend it as a part of your training routine. (See the section on breathing in chapter 9, Walking, and the section on meditation in chapter 10, The Ultralight State of Mind.) Each morning before doing anything else, meditate for fifteen minutes. The goal is to feel every sensation, every inner working of your body: the blood pumping through your veins, your stomach digesting, your muscles contracting, the breath moving in and out of your lungs. By becoming attuned to every single part of your

SUGGESTED GYM EXERCISES

EXERCISE	SETS	REPS.*	PURPOSE
ABDOMINALS			
Knee-in-air situps	2	15	Strengthen lower abdominals
Flat-bench leg raises	2	15	Strengthen upper abdominals
Crunches	2	UF**	Recruit smaller abdominals
LEGS			
Squats	4	10	Strengthen quads, hamstrings, calves
Leg presses	4	10	Variation of squat with more control
Seated calf raises	2	UF	Strengthen calves
Reverse calf pulls	2	UF	Strengthen front of calf muscle
BACK			
Deadlifts	4	10	Strengthen lower back
Hyperextensions	2	UF	Build mass around spine

* Repetitions.
** Until failure (i.e., you cannot physically perform an additional repetition).

body, you will be able to use it as efficiently as possible on the trail.

The training schedule is broken down by month, with physical exercises plus some thoughts on choosing gear and planning for food on the trail. The first three months are more physically demanding. By the end of that time, you will have strengthened all the muscles you will be using on the trail, and your cardiovascular system will be much improved. The purpose of the last three months is to adapt that extra muscle mass to the kind of exertion you will encounter on the trail.

It's important to stretch often. (See the section on stretching in chapter 8, Health and Safety.) Stretching helps prevent injury and frees up more muscle to be involved in whatever activity you are doing. At the gym, spend at least 10 minutes stretching all the muscles that you will be using. Stretch the larger muscles first. Start with the gluteus maximus (glutes) and quadriceps, then move to the hamstrings, calves, and groin muscles. Employ a stretching routine before running, bicycling, hiking, or other cardiovascular activities.

Month 1

Join a local gym and train using a weekly schedule that alternates gym exercises with activities that develop the cardiovascular system.

Monday: Gym
Tuesday: Short cardiovascular exercise (CE)
Wednesday: Gym
Thursday: Short CE
Friday: Gym
Saturday: Long CE
Sunday: Day off

For your cardiovascular exercise, pick an activity you feel comfortable with, such as running, biking, rowing, swimming, inline skating, or jumping rope. On the short CE days, continue the activity until your body starts offering resistance. On the long CE day, try to push through this sensation, and stop only when you reach an intolerable level of discomfort.

At left is a breakdown of suggested gym exercises. Start with 10 minutes on the exercise bike or treadmill, elevating your heart rate to 70 percent of maximum. Adjust your routine to accommodate any medical conditions you may have, and get advice from the trainers at the gym on the safest and most effective way to perform the exercises.

Gear. Focus on shoes, pack, tent, and sleeping bag, since these are the most critical items.

Visit backpacking retail stores and try on several different packs, filling them first with 30 to 40 pounds of weight. The store will have items you can use to simulate a loaded pack. This is much more weight than you will carry on the trail, but it accentuates any potential problem points on the pack.

When trying on shoes, stomp around in them enough to get a feel for any painful spots. Be sure the store accepts refunds for ill-fitting shoes, permitting you to buy a pair and to then spend a few hours walking in them. If they don't feel comfortable, exchange them for another pair.

Month 2

Monday: Gym
Tuesday: Short cardiovascular exercise (CE)
Wednesday: Gym
Thursday: 5-mile hike
Friday: Gym
Saturday: Long CE
Sunday: Day off

The routine for month 2 remains the same except for Thursday's 5-mile hike. Find terrain that is uneven and unpaved. By hiking uphill and downhill, you will strengthen different muscle and tendon groups. Carry a 30-pound pack throughout the training period, more than you will bear on the trail. The extra weight is to better condition your body so that when you finally strap on your trail pack, it will seem even more lightweight than it is. Use the same gym exercises as for month 1, but use heavier weight as your strength increases.

Gear. The Thursday hikes are partly to determine if the pack and shoes are just right for you. If you feel major soreness or pain that you are sure is due to the design of the pack or shoes, return the gear and find replacements. By the end of the month, you should have found a pack and shoes that fit perfectly. Once you decide on a pack that suits you, learn how to use every strap, buckle, and snap. Experiment with different settings to see which works the best.

You should also have a good idea of what shelter and sleeping bag you will be using. Begin writing a tentative list of other gear you will need, focusing research on the smaller essentials, including clothing, stove, cook pot, water containers, and first-aid kit.

Month 3

Monday: Gym
Tuesday: Short cardiovascular exercise (CE)
Wednesday: Gym
Thursday: 5-mile hike
Friday: Gym
Saturday: 10-mile hike
Sunday: Day off

The 10-mile hike is your first introduction to long-distance hiking as part of the training. Take it slow and easy, again carrying a 30-pound pack. The 10 miles should take you at least three hours, but not more than five. Take a 10-minute break every hour, no matter how strong you are feeling. Pack water and food for the hike, eating foods high in carbohydrates, such as dried fruit, candy bars, and energy bars (if you like them). Stretch every time you take a break.

Gear. By the end of this month, you should own the following: pack, shoes, shelter, sleeping bag, water containers, stove, fuel container, pot, first-aid kit, clothing, and maps. Know how to use each item, and how to repair it. Some gear is universally accepted as being the lightest and most efficient for the ultralight backpacker, but a lot of the gear you need has no such consensus. Research each piece of equipment before buying it, always keeping the weight factor at the front of your mind.

Food. You should be working on food issues now. The people on your e-mail list will offer plenty of advice, but take everything with a grain of salt, especially in regard to "legendary" food items. One person may like a certain energy bar that turns out to be not much better than dead weight in your pack. Everyone, it seems, has a different opinion. Jot down tentative meals and menus, but don't make any final decisions yet.

Month 4

Monday: 5-mile hike
Tuesday: Long cardiovascular exercise (CE)
Wednesday: Day off
Thursday: 5-mile hike
Friday: Day off
Saturday: 10-mile hike
Sunday: Day off

At this point you can cancel the gym membership—your muscular development should be more than enough for the trail. You will be hiking more now, conditioning muscles, tendons, and ligaments for the reality of the trail.

Sometime during the last week of this month, spend two days and one night on a backpacking trip, walking a total of 20 miles over the two days. You do not have to go far; in fact, you could camp in your backyard. But rely only on what you carry in your pack, and be sure to note every detail of the trip—physical sore points, problems with gear, what you needed but did not have, what you had but did not need, and so on.

Food. Make lists of menus, trying to be as precise as possible. If you wish, you can keep track of nutritional values of your chosen foods (carbohydrate, protein, and fat content). Begin planning your resupply strategy. Find a resupply coordinator, and begin assembling the boxes of food and other items to be sent to resupply points along the trail.

Month 5

Monday: 7-mile hike
Tuesday: Day off
Wednesday: 7-mile hike
Thursday: Day off
Friday: 12-mile hike
Saturday: Day off
Sunday: 7-mile hike

The focus of your training now is entirely on walking. Throughout the entire month, alternate a day of hiking with a day off. Simply extend the schedule above so that the second Monday is a rest day, and so forth. The idea is to begin racking up a lot of miles so that when you hit the trail and begin hiking 18 to 20 miles a day, day after day, your body will be quick to adapt and the hiking will be relatively pain-free.

Sometime during the last week of this month, take a three-day, two-night backpacking trip, hiking about 35 miles over the three-day period. Again, rely only on what you have in your pack, and make a note of absolutely every relevant detail of the trip.

Gear. You should now own every piece of equipment you will be taking with you. Carefully list everything, then weigh each item to monitor your efforts at stripping away every unnecessary ounce. Make sure that your resupply coordinator has full knowledge of each piece of equipment, in case he or she needs to send out a replacement.

Food. Make precise menus and calculate your daily nutritional intake. Plan and fill each resupply box, checking and rechecking that each box contains everything you need. Leave the boxes open so that you can add or remove items as needed.

Month 6

The last month doesn't have a strict schedule, concentrating instead on an overnight backpacking outing each week and a good bit of relaxation. Start the month by hiking 20 miles on pavement, carrying your pack. This will accentuate even the tiniest sore points you might have, so that you can correct any problems.

Once a week during this last month of training, go on a two-day, one-night backpacking trip, covering about 30 miles over the two days. Over the course of the six months of training, you should cover at least 350 miles. The higher the mileage, the more your body will be tuned to the lifestyle you will encounter on the trail.

Gear. Using the techniques you have learned in this book, every bit of weight should be trimmed from your equipment. Go over each item to see if there is any possible way to trim even more. Every last fraction of an ounce counts.

Food. Check and seal all resupply boxes, and then send the first three on their way. Make sure your resupply coordinator is perfectly clear on when to send the remaining boxes.

One Last Note. Your final month of training should be relatively relaxing. Try to make your life as simple as possible. By now, you will be thinking of nothing but the trail. While you are taking a shower, or eating breakfast, or driving to the local outdoors store for the thousandth time, your mind will already be at the trailhead. Most likely you will have last-minute moments of anxiety and fear, moments when you seem to understand as never before the concept of biting off more than you can chew. But these jitters will pass once you realize you've done absolutely everything in your control to fully prepare for life on the long-distance trail.

AN ULTRALIGHTER'S OVERNIGHT PACK

W E CAN NOW BRING TOGETHER EVERY-thing we've learned and apply it in planning what to take for a two-day, one-night ultralight backpacking trip. I've chosen items that meet the criteria we've studied throughout the chapters on gear and on food. My list represents one possible selection of items; in planning your own trip, choose whatever works best for you.

The list includes every item I'll take along, with each item's weight listed in ounces. Where I've reduced the weight of the item by trimming or other means, you'll find "AR" (after reduction) after the number. The asterisks indicate clothing that is worn while hiking and other items not part of the packweight.

PACK, SHELTER, SLEEPING BAG

Osprey Aether 36 backpack (35 AR ounces)
Sierra Designs Ultra Light Year one-person tent (37 AR)
Four right-angled titanium tent stakes (2 AR)
Western Mountaineering UltraLite sleeping bag (27 AR)
Therm-a-Rest UltraLite three-quarter-length sleeping pad (15)
Large waterproof garbage bag (1)
Pack and shelter: 7 lb., 5 oz.

CLOTHING

Patagonia Capilene thermal top (8 ounces*)
Patagonia Capilene thermal bottoms (6 AR)
Two pairs of Thor-Lo hiking socks (4*)
Extra pair of Thor-Lo hiking socks (4)
Patagonia R2 Levitator fleece pullover (13)
Mountain Hardwear Grade 5 waterproof jacket (9)
North Face nylon pants (14*)
Montrail Vitesse trail shoes (25*)
Fleece hat (2)
Fleece gloves (2)
Bandanna (2*)
Sun hat (3*)
Sunglasses (2*)
Eagle Creek Pack-It Compressor (1)
Clothing (excluding items worn): 2 lb., 5 oz.

COOKWARE

Snow Peak titanium GigaPower stove (3 ounces)
Snow Peak propane canister (5)
Small lighter (1 AR)
Evernew titanium 1-liter pot (7)
Lexan spoon (cut in half) (1 AR)
Two 2-liter Platypus water bladders (one with drinking hose) (4)
Ten iodine water-purification tablets (2)
Eagle Creek Pack-It Compressor (1)
Cookware: 1 lb., 8 oz.

HYGIENE

Tooth powder (1 ounce)
Toothbrush (cut in half) (1)
Dr. Bronner's liquid soap (in small Nalgene bottle) (3 AR)
Sunscreen (in small Nalgene bottle) (2 AR)
Insect repellent (in small Nalgene bottle) (2 AR)
Flannel hand towel (3)
Hygiene: 12 oz.

OTHER ITEMS

First-aid kit (7 ounces)
Map (1*)
Casio Pathfinder watch (compass, altimeter, barometer) (4*)
Mini Maglite (2)
25 feet of parachute cord (3)
Trekking poles (18*)
Duct tape (wrapped around trekking poles) (5*)
Leatherman Micro multitool (2)
Five waterproof matches (1)
Two birthday candles (1)
Other items (excluding items carried outside pack): 1 lb.
Subtotal (excluding food and water): 12 lb., 14 oz.

FOOD AND WATER

Water
Two liters

One Breakfast
1 Nutri-Grain bar
1 banana

Two Lunches
Beef jerky
Gorp (raisins, peanuts, M&Ms)
Dried fruit
4 Kraft cheese slices
12 Stone Wheat Thin crackers
2 Nature Valley granola bars
2 Sunkist fruit leathers

One Dinner
1 Lipton's noodles and sauce packet
1 can sweet corn (in zippered plastic bags)

Food and water: 6 lb., 9 oz.

TOTAL packweight: 19 lb., 9 oz.

* Indicates clothing that is worn and other items not counted in packweight

APPENDIX 2
MANUFACTURERS
AND SUPPLIERS

Adventure-lite Co.
www.adventurelite.com

Adventure Medical Kits
P.O. Box 43309
Oakland CA 94624
800-324-3517
www.adventuremedicalkits.com

Arc'teryx
4250 Manor St.
Burnaby BC V5G 1B2
CANADA
604-451-7755
www.arcteryx.com

Bibler Tents
2084 E. 3900 S.
Salt Lake City UT 84124
801-278-5552
www.biblertents.com

Cascade Designs
4000 1st Ave. S.
Seattle WA 98134
800-531-9531
www.cascadedesigns.com

Dana Design
25 S. Church Ave.
Bozeman MT 59715
406-585-9279
www.danadesign.com

Eagle Creek
1740 La Costa Meadows
San Marcos CA 92069
800-874-1048
www.eaglecreek.com

Edgeworks
8300 Military Road S.
Seattle WA 98108
800-550-8368
www.walrusgear.com

Feathered Friends
119 Yale Ave. N.
Seattle WA 98109
206-292-6292
www.featheredfriends.com

Frogg Toggs
517 Gunter Ave.
Guntersville AL 35976
800-349-1835
www.froggtoggs.com

GoLite
5785 Arapahoe
Boulder CO 80303
888-546-5483
www.golite.com

Gregory Mountain Products
100 Calle Cortez
Temecula CA 92590
800-477-3420
www.gregorypacks.com

Kelty Pack
6235 Lookout Road
Boulder CO 80301
800-423-2320
www.kelty.com

Leki USA
356 Sonwil Drive
Buffalo NY 14225
800-255-9982
www.leki.com

Marmot Mountain Ltd.
2321 Circadian Way
Santa Rosa CA 95407
707-544-4590
www.marmot.com

Merrell Performance Footwear
9341 Courtland Drive
Rockford MI 49351
888-637-7001
www.merrellboot.com

Montrail
1003 6th Ave. S.
Seattle WA 98134
800-826-1598
www.montrail.com

Moonstone Mountain Equipment
833 Indiana St.
San Francisco CA 94107
800-390-3312
www.moonstone.com

Mountain Hardwear
950-A Gilman St.
Berkeley CA 94710
800-330-6800
www.mountainhardwear.com

Mountain Safety Research
P.O. Box 24547
Seattle WA 98124
800-877-9677
www.msrcorp.com

Mountainsmith
18301 W. Colfax Ave.
Heritage Square, Bldg. P
Golden CO 80401
800-551-5889
www.mountainsmith.com

The North Face
2013 Farallon Dr.
San Leandro CA 94577
800-447-2333
www.thenorthface.com

Only the Lightest Camping
   Equipment
www.hikelight.com

Osprey Packs
P.O. Box 539
Dolores CO 81323
970-564-5900
www.ospreypacks.com

Outdoor Research
2203 First Ave. S.
Seattle WA 98134-1424
888-467-4327
www.orgear.com

Pack Lite Foods
www.packlitefoods.com

Patagonia
239 W. Santa Clara St.
Ventura CA 93001
800-638-6464
www.patagonia.com

Petzl America
P.O. Box 160447
Clearfield UT 84016
801-327-3805
www.petzl.com

PUR Drinking Water Systems
9300 N. 75th Ave.
Minneapolis MN 55428
800-845-7873
www.purwater.com

Rain Shield
5110A Cedar Lake Road
Minneapolis MN 55416
952-543-1894
www.rainshield.com

Sierra Designs
1255 Powell St.
Emeryville CA 94608
800-635-0461
www.sierradesigns.com

Snow Peak USA
4754 Avery Lane
Lake Oswego OR 97035
503-697-3330
www.snowpeak.com

Tom Harrison Maps
2 Falmouth Cove
San Rafael CA 94901
800-265-9090
www.tomharrisonmaps.com

Ursack
P.O. Box 5002
Mill Valley CA 94942
866-232-7224
www.ursack.com

Wanderlust Outdoor Gear
www.wanderlustgear.com

Western Mountaineering
1025 S. Fifth St.
San Jose CA 95112
408-287-8944
*www.westernmountaineering.
   com*

APPENDIX 3
WORLD WIDE WEB RESOURCES

PERSONAL ULTRALIGHT WEB SITES

Joe's Ultralight Backpacking
www.ultralightbackpacker.com
A solid overview with information on philosophy, gear, and food, and links to trip reports.

Lightweight Backpacker
www.backpacking.net
Easily the most comprehensive ultralight Web site, with message boards, gear lists and reviews, ultralight writings, and a store.

Michael's Ultralight Backpacking Page
www.monmouth.com/~mconnick
Innovative ideas on clothing, great personal ultralight experiences, and good list of links.

Onestep's Ultralight Backpacking Resource
http://onestep4me.tripod.com
Good informantion on homemade gear, plus personal trip reports.

Ray Jardine's Adventure Page
www.rayjardine.com/index.shtml
Ideas on ultralight and a slew of other pursuits by a founding father of ultralight backpacking.

Ultralight Hiking.com
http://ultralight-hiking.com/home.html
A thorough site with extensive gear reviews.

MAILING LISTS AND MESSAGE BOARDS

www.backpacking.net/bbs.html
www.egroups.com/subscribe.cgi/backpacking light

LINKS TO HOMEMADE GEAR

Fabriclink's Product Knowledge Center
www.fabriclink.com/pk/x-camping.html

Make Your Own Gear
www.backpacking.net/makegear.html

Sierra Solid Fuel Stove
www.gorp.com/zzstove/sierra.htm

Three Fuel Stove
www.monmouth.com/~mconnick/stove.htm

LONG-DISTANCE THRU-HIKING

American Long Distance Hikers Association
www.aldha.org

American Long Distance Hikers Association
  West
www.gorp.com/nonprof/aldhaw

Appalachian Trail Homepage
www.fred.net/kathy/at.html

AT Trailplace for Thru-Hikers
www.trailplace.com

Appalachian Trail Conference
www.atconf.org

Continential Divide Trail Society
www.gorp.com/cdts

Pacific Crest Trail Association
www.pcta.org

PCT Planning Program
www.newestindustry.com/pct/pctplan

MISCELLANEOUS

Plantar Fasciitis
www.heelspurs.com/_intro.html
Information on plantar fasciitis, an inflammation of tissue on the bottom of the foot.

INDEX

Photo Credits

Trademarks